"Calvin has developed
all those wanting to kn
places that are 'Must
miss in and around Mou............."
—Jessica Roberts, Executive Director of Tourism, Chairman
of the Triad Film Association, President of the Blue Ridge
Association, and Board Member of 13 State Southeast
Tourism Association

"My cousin, Calvin, has written a must-read about my
hometown."
—Donna Fargo, Grammy-winning singer-songwriter,
author, and winner of five Academy of Country Music and
one Country Music Association awards.

"Calvin Vaughn has captured the heart of my hometown.
Read it – you will be blessed. I treasure growing up in the
small town of Mount Airy. I would not trade it for anything,
that is why I moved my store to Main Street."
—James Easter, two-time Dove Award winner, an original
member of the Easter Brothers, author of 400 published
songs

"In the book, Life on MAin, Calvin shares his passionate
belief that small town Mount Airy, NC mirrors the spirit of
Mayberry."
—Dustin Stephens, Producer, CBS Sunday Morning

"Mount Airy is one of our time's great promotional stories,
and Calvin Vaughn is one of its amiable salesmen. Enjoy the
ride."
—Ted Koppel, Author, and host of *Nightline*

Life on MAin

Look for **Mayberry ABCs** and
Mortimer Goes to Mayberry –
two new children's books released in early 2023.

Watch for More Titles
from Calvin B. Vaughn, Jr.

and *Life on MAin Publishing*

Life on MAin

the Heart and Soul of America.

Calvin B. Vaughn, Jr.

Life on MAin Publishing
Mount Airy, North Carolina

Life on MAin
lifeonmain@yahoo.com

The opinions expressed in this work are entirely the opinions of the author. The author has represented and warranted all ownership and/or legal right to publish all the materials in this book.

First Life on MAin edition published
October 2021
Life on MAin Publishing, Logo, and all production design are trademarks.

For information regarding bulk purchases of this book, digital purchases, and special discounts, please contact the publisher at
600 Merritt Street, Mount Airy NC 27030
lifeonmain@yahoo.com
Books are available in quantity for group studies.
Contact the author for a private tour, group tour, or motivational speaker.
lifeonmain@yahoo.com

Cover photo, left to right: Jonathan Lightfoot, Nelson Montalvo, Linda Shubert, Bret Harris, Lillian Montalvo, Edith Thomas, Amy Heath, Paul McCraw, Calvin Vaughn, and Jim Reeves

Cover design by Geoffrey Walker
Manufactured in the United States of America
ISBN 978-1-63066-529-6

Dedication

This book is dedicated to my wonderful family who has supported, inspired and given me unconditional love. The heritage from my parents, Calvin and Kitty Vaughn, and grandmothers Esther Reynolds and Maude Vaughn, made me who I am today. They have always believed in me. My sisters Sybil Vaughn Guyer, and Carol Vaughn, both have given me strength that helped in my journey. They have also given me wonderful nieces and nephews. And of course, my special friend Nora adds richness to all I do.

Heather Elliot was valuable in editing; she knows my spirit. Mike Simpson, owner of Empower Publishing provided personal advice and professional services that enabled me to put my passion into print. Thank you.

—**Calvin B. Vaughn, Jr.**

Calvin and Nora at the outdoor concert at Blackmon Amphitheatre

CONTENTS

Preface

The popularity of Mayberry brings more than a million people to Mount Airy (population of just over 10,000) each year. From across the country and all over the world, people come looking for an idyllic town popularized on *The Andy Griffith Show* as Mayberry. They are searching for traditions, morals, values, and charm. They are seeking community, connection, and a slower pace of life. And while Mayberry may be fictional, Mount Airy is very real.

Real people were my inspiration for this book. Come take a walk down Main Street and meet the kinds of people who make this town such a wonderful place to live. Their neighborliness and just good living will warm your heart, revive your spirit, and stir your emotions. They will inspire you to be the best person you can be.

Calvin B. Vaughn Jr.

People make up a town, and you won't find any better people than the ones you'll meet here.

Welcome to Main Street, Mount Airy, North Carolina! We're so glad you stopped by. Have a seat, there are some folks I'd like you to meet...

—Calvin

Calvin B. Vaughn, Jr.

How to Use This Book

First, *Life on MAin* is a collection of true stories that are written for an easy and enjoyable read, honoring the people who make small-town America great.

Each captivating story inspires and uncovers loads of interesting details and amazing facts you never knew about our small town.

The **Things to Do in Mount Airy** section in Appendix I provides the most exhaustive list of tourist sites and areas of interest that have been written in one book.

The abundant tourist information listed in Appendix II **More on MAin** and Appendix III **Beyond MAin** provides *the most inclusive informational guide for touring Mount Airy.*

The **Famous People from Mount Airy** section in Appendix IV lists more than 50 people (and their accomplishments) from our small town who made America a better place.

The **Reflections** section in Appendix V provides an opportunity for devotionals and group studies.

The information contained here was accurate as of publication, on October 15, 2021. I will make every effort to keep current information available going forward.

Trinity Episcopal, 1895

Oldest Granite Church on Main Street

Blessed...Jim Reeves

"AGAIN, this was a great year." He repeated so many times in the book that it felt comfortable, like wearing a favorite pair of old shoes.

My Way, an autobiography, is an honest and warm synopsis of the life of Jimmy (Jim) Reeves. He shines with an appreciation for being an American, recognizing that the land of the free provides life choices and opportunities to succeed. In the pages of the book, Jim proclaims he is blessed. His life affirms it.

Mindful of the love that surrounded his childhood, he is thankful. Most of all, he appreciates how blessed he is to have his own experience of building a family with love. The 47-year educator acknowledges how education and religion gave hope. He recalls, "What a wonderful and blessed life I've lived."

After reading his book, two things echoed in my mind: first, how grateful he is for all the blessings in his life; and next, the depth of lifelong friendships he has developed.

In 1938, he was born in a log cabin on a small farm in the Holy Springs community (five miles south of Mount Airy). A cool spring near the house served as the refrigerator and was the source of water for cooking and bathing. There was a large, fruitful garden; chickens pecked around the yard; pigs rooted in their pen; and cows roamed in the pasture. Nonessentials were rare and extra garments were uncommon. For example, growing up, he had one pair of new shoes per year. "We were materially dirt poor," he remembers, "but rich in spirit."

For the first few years, the family lived next to his grandparents. When he was five, they moved to the Flat Rock community (a few miles east of Mount Airy). (see Appendix III Beyond MAin...Communities and Towns in

Surry County)

A clear factor attributing to Jim's good character is his laudable lineage.

His mother, Mattie Simmons Reeves, was the daughter of kind and gentle parents. No doubt, the roots of her graceful ability to discipline with love were inherited from them. For those who knew his mother, there was not enough good that could be said about her. At age 15, the assiduous, hardworking woman began to toil in hosiery mills and continued until she retired at 65. Everyone loved her and many would say she was always thinking of others. She lived to the age of 100.

Jim's father, John William Reeves, disciplined with love through strict expectations. He was an industrious man, building their Flat Rock home by hand. When it was destroyed by fire, he said, "I will build it again." And he did. His dad's hard work, as a State employee in the road division, was rewarded with a promotion to a supervisory position. Active in the community, he served on the School Board. Sadly, Jim's dad developed a heart condition and died when Jim was a young man.

One of his best friends is his sister, Pat. She has always been supportive. He could always talk to her about anything. "She gives great advice," he says.

Jim grew up in simpler times, with two community hangouts: the church and the Flat Rock Texaco. Socially, they were equally important, places where lifelong friendships were built.

The church filled with youth activities kept the neighborhood boys and girls busy and out of trouble. It provided great role models.

The Flat Rock Texaco was a gas station, a grocery store, and Jim's favorite hangout during his teen years. It was the gathering place for friends, especially when you had a dime. With the coin, you felt on top of the world and gathered your friends like a mother hen gathers her chicks. Then off to the store to share your riches with your buddies.

Most families in the community had limited finances. Sometimes, they had to use credit for things they could not grow or make. The store owner (a neighbor) allowed folks to pay when they got the money. In that era, people knew their neighbors, more people felt responsible, and almost everyone paid their bills.

During adolescence, Jim experienced two watershed events. First, the polio epidemic in the1950s. Uncertain how the virus was spread, fear-filled most homes. Public places closed, and children were kept home during the historic time of social distancing. The memories are vivid in his mind, but true to his nature, he chooses to focus on happier times.

The second momentous event is the era of the All-American Soapbox Derby (a race for children with motorless improvised vehicles). The racing started in 1933. In its heyday, Jim and his friends raced on the big hill on Spring Street, near downtown.

One year, he won big. The first-place title provided an opportunity for him to advance. The with n, first of many, made him feel on top of the world. After qualifying, his family and buddies traveled to Winston-Salem for the next round of races. It was the biggest day of his young life.

Wide as saucers, his eyes surveyed the race site. He had never seen anything as grand. As he gazed at the hundreds of seats at the stadium, his heart revved like a brand-new engine. People were everywhere. He watched the cars launch from the starting point, the wheels turning faster and faster until they seemed to travel with the speed of an eagle. With confidence, he anxiously waited his turn.

Winning first place again, the young boy with humble beginnings felt success. A feeling repeated time after time throughout his life.

Recorded in the local newspaper, he competed against 140 racers. Headlines on the sports page read "Mechanic's

Son Wins Soapbox Derby". It was a news flash on TV and the story spread all over the Flat Rock community. The win qualified him for the national competition.

Jim, along with the sports editor, was flown to Akron, Ohio. After arriving, they were escorted by police to the Derby Downs. This was the first of many exciting events experienced over his lifetime.

Continuing to shine in high school, Jim was inducted into the Beta Club. The Club educates and develops youth to be leaders. He was honored by representing the school on trips. One of the bigger honors was developing friendships. The sponsoring teacher of the Club would become a colleague and lifelong friend.

Active in school, he had many friends, as well as a close circle of friends. They elected him as the senior class president. His priority was sports. He was a great athlete in the backyard and on the school field. He committed to being the best athlete he could be. A sportswriter with *The Elkin Newspaper* wrote, "Jim is one of the cleverest ball handlers I have ever seen."

The passionate sportsman played all types of sports, but during his professional career, he develop a love for tennis. And true to his nature to make things happen, he started a tennis program at Surry Community College and led the team to several impressive wins. (see Appendix III Beyond MAin...Surry Community College)

He developed into an outstanding community leader. In 1954, Hank Schofield, Sports Editor with the *Journal and Sentinel* wrote, "It is a great pleasure to know the Reeves family...Jimmy is a fine boy." Similar affirmations were repeated many times in his life by neighbors, classmates, workers, and professional acquaintances, all of whom would become enduring friends.

After high school, and a brief, insipid encounter with college, Jim joined the Air Force. He met people from all over the country and made lifelong friends.

Born with confidence and an adventurous spirit, he always wanted to be the best. He has never been afraid to face challenges. He believes positive change can happen, he believes he can help make it happen, and he is fierce in the quest.

He could have been the originator of the "art of the deal". He loves trading cars. His lifetime affair with trading four wheels and a body began with his first vehicle, a 1950 Chevy. He says cars have always been his Achilles Hill.

Car trading was a hobby, but he would do what needed to be done to make a living and care for his wife and family. Since he was a young boy, Jim has been a hardworking person. On his path to becoming a professional educator, he worked at freight lines and hosiery mills. Doing what needed to be done never deterred his focus to become the best he could be in a professional setting.

As a young man, he searched for greatness. Being a visionary, he knew there was more. He developed a healthy desire to succeed. Although his first step to college was less than successful, he eventually went to Appalachian State College and made the Dean's List in the first quarter.

It was during those college years that he met his best friend of all time. Her name is Gayle and early in their relationship, they connected in a special way. It was a whirlwind romance. They married, uniting to build a wonderful life.

Gayle became his greatest supporter, calming comforter, endless encourager, and an integral part of every decision and every success. She is an exceptional human being, and well accomplished by her own merits. The title of her autobiography could be *The Hand That Held It All Together.*

Among the couple's many achievements, they would say they are most proud of their three beautiful and successful daughters, Leigh Ann, Mary Beth, and Jayme. Jim wanted to be the best dad there was, and he obtained his desire.

Working full-time, managing a household, and

successfully parenting three children is a full-time job and a great achievement for any man or woman. Yet, he and Gayle were self-disciplined and pursued higher education to obtain greater life goals. He earned a doctorate, and she earned a degree in Special Education. Swanson Richards, Surry Community College's second president, and a 25-year colleague of his said, "Jim Reeves is the most self-disciplined person I have ever met."

Jim's commitment to education coupled with his determination to be the best in his profession led to early career successes. First, teaching in Winston-Salem, and then he secured a position at Campbell College.

When the occasion arose, he seized the opportunity to enter the doors of Surry Community College. He knew he wanted to work toward being president and his decision proved to be advantageous. The initial step into a position at the campus led to a 32-year career at the community college. He began with a contract to coordinate a new Federal Vocational Program and served as a part-time counselor in charge of student financial aid.

In a few years, he advanced to the position of the Dean of Continuing Education. After impressive achievements, he was awarded the position of Dean of Student Services, a position that expanded his responsibilities. He continued the ascending road to fulfilled professional achievement with an appointment to be Vice-President of Instruction. After four years, the Board installed him as President of Surry Community College. With great gratitude, Jim had climbed to the summit of his professional goal as a lifelong educator.

His powerful connections aided him in accomplishing many things for the college and his career. A few of his numerous accomplishments include the construction of the Richards Health Science Building; the construction of a Fireman and Law Enforcement Facility; the development of a satellite campus in Yadkin County; the implementation of technology necessary to network the campus; a revision of faculty salaries and he organized the first foundational golf tournament providing scholarships for students.

Jim suggests that good timing and luck play a role in success. I agree, but I believe his serving in excellence is the main contributor to his accomplishments.

He started at the college when the school was not much more than an idea. He was part of the community college throughout its growing years. His desire to see underprivileged students succeed led him to design an academic developmental plan for underprepared students. He said, "The most rewarding part of my involvement is seeing the people come with a need and go to their lives more successful."

He witnessed firsthand how shattered lives could be repaired and how young people on destructive paths could set new directions. He helped hundreds of struggling students obtain a better life. He recognized that "Surry Community College is a refuge for many people." With thanksgiving, Jim feels extremely blessed to be a part of how the community college experience has mended the broken lives of many.

Dr. Reeves' profound wisdom aided him in his professional successes. He wisely studied behavior and relationships. He said, "I learned that the basis for all behavior is rooted in a person's self-concept." He believes in "being accepting and non-judgmental" with positive reinforcement. His wisdom, inner drive, and education were crowned with blessings.

Crowning the accomplishment of his professional career, The Appalachian State University's Reich College of Education inducted Jim into the Rhododendron Society. The prestigious society recognizes outstanding professional alumni educators who demonstrate remarkable and exemplary accomplishments. Only a few alumni receive this honor each year.

After retiring, Dr. Reeves reached even further to transform lives. He accepted a position as Coordinator for Appalachian Learning Alliance, building the program, he expanded it to ten community colleges. He continued in this position for 12 years. The program helped alleviate teacher shortages and helped start master's degree programs in community colleges.

He was asked to return to Surry Community College as interim president and played a leading role in securing the next president.

Humbly aware, with thanksgiving, Jim understands he is a favored man. Acknowledging his gifts in life and career, he began to give to others through community service. He served on the Mount Airy School Board, the Social Services Board, and the Board of Trustees for the Northern Surry Hospital.

Currently, he serves on the Pro-Health Board of Directors, continues to teach Sunday School (he has been doing it for 40 years) and he has served as Sunday School superintendent at the largest granite church in Mount Airy. He brought positive results to the community by participating on numerous other boards and committees. (see Appendix II More on MAin...Granite Churches on Main)

Always an athlete, Jim's desire to remain physically active led him to begin a running program many years ago. He logged four miles a day, five days a week for 40 years. During that time, he registered 10,000 days of running for a total of 40,000 miles. He ran in the first 5k Race on the Greenway hosted by Mount Airy Parks and Recreation. He continues to be active by walking four miles per day. (see Appendix III Beyond MAin...Greenway)

Outdoor activities allow the octogenarian to remain physically active. In the past year, he added another sport to his active schedule: pickleball (the fastest-growing sport in America). (see Appendix III Beyond MAin...Outdoor Recreation and Beyond MAin...Pickleball Courts)

Pickleball is the door that led to my friendship with Jim. I met him when he was beginning to embrace the game. Being an exceptionally good tennis player, he quickly learned the new game. In a few weeks, he was playing competitively.

Recognizing he was a good man, I immediately connected with his good nature. I discovered we were linked by our past. He went to school with my dad, and he is a good friend of my cousin Yvonne Vaughn (who is known worldwide as Donna Fargo). (see Appendix III Beyond MAin...Donna Fargo)

I enjoyed talking with Jim and hearing about the former days,

Jim Playing Pickleball

but most of all I enjoyed getting to know him. I count it an honor to have become one of his friends. I understand why my family connected with him and I see why people build lifelong friendships with him. He is an honorable man.

It is easy to see all the good things in Jim's life, but he says his greatest two blessings are his family and his lifelong friends. What a testament.

Jim said, repeatedly, when telling his story, "Again, it was a good year." I would like to modify that statement so we can all use it: Every year is a good year when you acknowledge your blessings.

Looking through the years, and studying the lives of other people, I have noticed a couple of truths appear over and over. Thankful people enjoy life and blessed people who bless others are more blessed.

There are many blessed people in our small town.

This vignette is based on the notes taken by the writer from Jim's autobiography <u>My Way</u> and compiled from conversations and personal interactions with Jim.

Calling...Melvin Miles

Just as he was awakened to his calling, his heart was broken.

In rural Allegany County in 1949, visitors were allowed in the schoolroom that was warmed during cold mountain winters by a potbellied stove. Little Melvin was a frequent visitor.

Not old enough to register for school, he often attended the classroom as his older cousin's guest. He cherished his time at school, not caring that there were not enough chairs for everyone to sit on. Sometimes, he had to sit on a bench pushed up against the wall.

He loved learning. With a hunger to absorb information, he exceeded the grade level of the older students. The teacher, concerned that the preschool lad was advancing ahead of the enrolled pupils, ended his visits. For a boy so enamored of learning, it was heartbreaking.

But that little, heartbroken boy did not despair for long. Confined to home, he created his own schoolhouse with imaginary friends. Of course, due to his natural leadership qualities, he appointed himself as the teacher.

Playschool was fun but waiting to go to "real" school felt like one of the longest years of his life.

Finally, the morning arrived. The first-grade boy was thrilled. Melvin vividly recalls jumping out of bed and racing to get dressed. He says he may have swallowed his breakfast with one gulp, he was in such a hurry to gather his things and dash out the door to wait for the bus. He was all smiles when he saw the big yellow cocoon on wheels that would carry him to the place he prized.

He was the happiest boy in school that day. More than prepared, he knew the alphabet and how to count. Recognizing his advanced level of knowledge, the teacher put him in front of the class to help the other students.

It was a natural place for him. Standing in front of the classroom fit Melvin like a glove. He continued to assist his schoolmates for the rest of the year. He enjoyed helping them learn. Glowing with good memories, the grown man remembers, "I was so proud. I felt in charge."

Music was a part of the opening of every school day, and being from a musical family, Melvin had the ability to fill another leadership void. By the second grade, he directed the daily song having been elected by the other students to be the "song leader." It was an honor for which he was incredibly grateful. He filled the role for the next seven years, and by the eighth grade, he was playing the piano for all the school programs. His calling was becoming clearer and clearer.

In high school, he had a business teacher who influenced the direction his life took. Her profound impact helped him to clarify his calling even more. He would go to college and enter the world of education. However, a degree in Business Education would take money the family did not have. Throughout high school, he worked and saved money for education. Once he was attending college, he continued to work and pay his way until he graduated from Appalachian State Teacher's College.

In his junior college year, Melvin was tempted by a profitable offer that would have steered him away from his calling. A Duke University professor heard about his impressive business skills, especially typing. The professor dangled a job opportunity that would have put him in charge of a group of people in the business world. He was guaranteed to be paid much more money than a teacher's salary. Although he was honored by the offer, he remained focused on his calling.

In his final college year, he took the big step of student teaching. The experience was an eye-opener. He came from a high school class of 67 graduates to a small college environment. He was assigned to a high school of over 1600 students. He was stunned to learn he had five classes and a total of 227 students to teach. Furthermore, he became flummoxed with the unconventional student teaching method.

The normal path for an intern teacher was first to observe, then gradually build the classroom load by adding one class per week till the student teacher had a full day of teaching experience (being monitored the whole time). After practicing teaching for two weeks, with a full teaching schedule, the intern would begin to drop one class each week until there were no more classes (again while being monitored). After successfully completing the routine approach, the student teacher was eligible for certification. Shockingly, Melvin was given the full load the first day and kept it the whole time. He was also without a monitor the entire time.

Although he managed to complete his unusual student teaching successfully, the intense experience further clarified his mission. He wanted to teach in a small school where he could become better acquainted with the students. He thought it was important to get to know the students, it made it easier to teach. He said, "My philosophy is to teach the student, not just teach the subject."

That philosophy defined his career and made an enormous impact on numerous students Melvin taught over the years.

His first day as a certified teacher, in a new school, was exciting. He felt comfortable meeting the full staff of 14 teachers. Immediately, after the cordial introductions, the teachers began voicing disparaging statements about a particular student. Some said he was easily angered, others that thought he had a bad temper. One warned, "he has been known to physically strike teachers." In concert, they hoped that the novice teacher would not get the problem student in his classroom.

Melvin was shocked, thinking on the way to the classroom, "What have I got myself into?"

Addressing his first class of the morning with apprehension, Mr. Miles directed the students to stand one at a time, state their names, and share something about themselves. The first student to stand was a tall, good-looking young man. With a normal tone, he proceeded to say, "I like sports. I play football, basketball, and baseball." Then he said his name. Melvin was speechless. It was the student the other teachers had warned him about.

As the day went on, Mr. Miles learned that he would have the boy in all five classes. As if by fate, he was the young man's only teacher that year.

Sticking to his philosophy, though, Melvin had quite a different experience with him than the other teachers. The first-year teacher formed a meaningful relationship with the underprivileged juvenile. At the end of the school year, the student visited Melvin asking for advice. It had become commonplace to talk with him because he knew that Mr. Miles cared. Melvin discussed options with his student, all the while emphasizing the need for further education. The young man decided to go into military service, and took his teacher's advice, beginning college coursework while in service.

In a few years, the young man was teaching. He later became a principal in the small county where he grew up. He became an outstanding educator, developing the curriculum for the early college program for the state of North Carolina. In addition to his successful career in education, he was also elected mayor of the same small town where he grew up.

While others had looked down on the boy, Melvin had seen the potential. He became a major influence in helping the young man become successful in school and life. It was the first of many lifelong significant relationships Mr. Miles would foster with his students. His calling became even more clear, and he became known for being a positive transformational influence on the lives of troubled youth. He focused his career on it.

After teaching for a few years, he moved to Mount Airy and joined the staff at the high school as the Industrial Cooperative Training Coordinator. He said it was a "very rewarding job." While he was at Mount Airy, he had a student named Todd Jessup.

Todd shared with me his admiration for his favorite teacher. "You could talk to him," Todd said, "he would always help you." Todd credits his success to the support he received from Mr. Miles, saying that he taught life lessons as well as school subjects, and always showed compassion. Todd went on to teach, too, as well as fulfill his dream of becoming a radio disc jockey.

There are countless examples of other students who attribute the direction and success of their life to Mr. Miles.

Melvin had a full and successful teaching career. While still in his first year as an educator, he was so zealous about being in the classroom that he started teaching night classes in the community college as well. For the remainder of his teaching profession, he taught both day and night. During his career as a high school educator, he also taught in three community colleges and for the North Carolina State Extension Services.

Staying faithful to his calling and gift to connect with disadvantaged students, he was recruited to be the Coordinator of an alternative school for troubled youth. Under Melvin's leadership, the program became a model for the State of North Carolina.

During his vocation, and without campaigning, he was voted in as a member of the first elected school board in Mount Airy. After retirement, the "called" educator went on to develop 15 alternative school programs around the state.

A calling never concludes but only transitions. In retirement, Melvin has been busy as an author, lecturer, and tour guide.

He wrote *From Siam to Surry* about Eng and Chang Bunker, the Original Siamese Twins. They traveled from Siam (now Thailand) to America in the 1800s and settled in Surry County. He lectures on the topic for various organizations and audiences. (see Appendix III Beyond MAin...Siamese Twins)

Melvin worked as a guide for Mayberry Squad Car Tours for 16 years. In this different educational setting, he continued to share his wealth of knowledge, this time with interesting facts about Mount Airy, Andy Griffith, the Granite Quarry, and more. As a guide, he hosted people from all 50 states, local and national government officials, newspaper and magazine reporters, television personalities, and many cast members of *The Andy Griffith Show.* (see Appendix II More on MAin...Wally's Service Station and Squad Car Tours)

Recently, Melvin began serving as a guide for the Mount Airy Visitors Center. (see Appendix II More on MAin...Mount Airy Visitors Center)

Once, while having a conversation with Melvin, we discussed his love of teaching. He said, "I suppose that I have the gift of gab." While he certainly does, I think there is a lot more to it than that. Another time we were talking, he remarked, "I have such a love for people, and I love to share with them. I guess I will work until two days before being placed six feet under. I have been very blessed in being able to touch so many lives of people from all ages and lots of areas geographically. For that, I can only be grateful to God for presenting me with these treasured opportunities."

On January 25, 2020, he celebrated his 77th birthday. He received over 500 birthday wishes from former students, some he taught in the 1960s. It is evident, with a commitment to his calling, hundreds of people have been influenced by this teacher who genuinely cared.

The first hint of his calling was seen in his childhood

school visits. Signs continued throughout his school years until it became clear. With determination and focus, he fulfilled his destiny by answering his calling.

You too have been given hints and signs to help identify your call. Appreciate the clues. Discover and answer your calling.

Countless people, in our small town, have answered their calling.

Melvin Miles
Driving a Squad Car

Melvin passed in February 2023

Calm...Ken White

The superstar had expectations. His requests had been met.

On the day of the performance, everything that could go wrong went wrong. The show had been scheduled for over a year, and now it was show time. The facilities manager had done everything right, but the soundboard and the spotlight technology were not as dependable.

The line of excited patrons backed up; the crowd was restless. The aroma of popcorn wafted around the theatergoers as they bumped against each other maneuvering through the small lobby.

The aisles of the 1930s music hall filled as fans frantically packed the seats, everyone hoping the show was not delayed. Some anxiously scanned the walls for a clock, others glared at their phones, and several people peered at their watch.

Questions sprayed like buckshot from all directions; patrons, staff, and volunteers all had requests, and some had demands. The hectic environment and the potential for disaster would rattle most people, but Ken White calmly remained as in control of the situation as possible as Plan B gently glided through his mind.

If sound and lights could not be coaxed to work, where would he move 400 people at the last minute? With a calm focus that flowed like a peaceful stream and a gentle spirit that could soothe a roaring lion, Ken was unruffled. Composed and unflustered, he calmly addressed every question and resolved every issue.

Only a few minutes late, to the delight of the audience and the superstar, the lights went up, the sound came on and the show began. Barely a ripple of emotion could be seen on the kindhearted face of Ken, all was well and there was no need for Plan B.

He began working with the Surry Arts Council (SAC) thirty-five years ago. SAC had lost their janitor, and Brack Lewellyn (an employee at the time) asked him if he would come and sweep.

Today, he is the Facilities Manager and oversees four properties: The Historic Earle Theatre, The Andy Griffith Museum, the Andy Griffith Playhouse, and the Blackmon Amphitheatre. (See Appendix III Beyond MAin...Surry Arts Council)

The 438-seat Earle Theatre was built in 1938. In addition to hosting concerts, radio broadcasts, and music lessons and showing feature films, it is the home of two major exhibits: The Old-Time Music Heritage Hall and the Women in Surry County Old-Time Music exhibit.

The Andy Griffith Museum has the largest collection of Griffith memorabilia in the world. The museum has expanded to include a special exhibit on actress (and local resident) Betty Lynn who played Thelma Lou on the show.

The Andy Griffith Playhouse, circa 1920, is the former school auditorium where Andy first performed on stage as a boy in elementary school. It continues to stage community theatre productions as well as school programming for all the schools in the county.

The Blackmon Amphitheatre is a state-of-the-art outdoor theater that hosts the SAC's Summer Music Series featuring Beach and R&B music from April through October.

Occasionally, Ken still sweeps, but his responsibilities have expanded like a blowout at an oil well, gushing endlessly. He is the "fixer," on a tight budget; he puts patch on patch to keep things operating. He builds sets for stage shows, works the soundboard, handles the lights, takes care of any facility need, and is often the first contact for performing artists arriving in town.

With over 500 performances each year, his responsibilities seem endless, and the potential for stressful situations are innumerable. Yet, always, he is calm.

The first time I met him, I observed his meek temperament, peaceful nature, and humble spirit. It was a pleasure to meet him. He has the type of spirit you admire and enjoy being around. As a regular attendee of the local performing arts, I continued to see him frequently. At all four venues, at almost every show, I would see him, discreetly handling multiple tasks, assuring the shows would go on.

The appearance of meekness is deceptive. Some people mistakenly think a meek person is weak – but the opposite is true. A person calmly in control while maintaining a meek spirit is one of the strongest people you will ever know.

During stressful times, in the face of adversity, it takes giant strength to be meek and remain calm. Calm meekness has choices – out-of-control anger does not. Recognizing his strength, I wondered, "How does one become meek or develop a spirit of calmness?"

One afternoon at the Earle Theatre, during the showing of the weekly movie, Ken and I had time for a heart-to-heart in the lobby. I shared my appreciation for his kindness and humble spirit. As our discussion continued and I unwrapped the origin and source of his meekness, I had a surprise.

I discovered his grandfather was Reverend Porter Cockerham. I remember Preacher Cockerham from when I was a teenager. He was one of the humblest men I have ever met. Most everyone admired his gentle spirit. I could see a personality resemblance between Ken and his grandfather, and the similarity made me ponder how personalities are developed.

Our personalities are formed both from our DNA imprint and our relationship to our environment. Therefore, I think whom we become evolves from both biological and environmental factors.

I see my theory confirmed in Ken's heritage and the relationship he had with his grandfather. He said, "My grandfather was an amazing man. He knew the answer to everything. He had kind words for everyone, and he always had time to listen. He shaped my life."

While remembering his grandfather, his voice began to break, and tears filled his eyes. Choking with emotion, it took a couple of moments before he could talk. Lovingly, he continued to describe his saintly grandfather.

"When my grandfather's children would pay their dad a compliment, he would cry," Ken shared. He further revealed that his grandfather made people feel valued. He did not draw attention to himself or dominate a conversation unless there was a grave injustice about to take place, then he would boldly speak up in defense of the offended person. Ken acts and responds the same way.

He went on to describe his parents, "Both, my parents and my grandfather taught me a lot." He shared that one of the best things they taught him was to value other people. They imparted morals such as integrity and respect. They taught him how to be a giving person.

He especially values one lesson they taught him, which is showing honor to another person. The way that looks in daily living is "preferring" one another (Romans 12:10). When you prefer one another, you let the person know how important you think they are and how much you value them. It is a way of showing equality. No one is better than anyone else.

Our DNA may stamp good traits into us, but our influences help us to choose to live humbly and strive to grow meeker. Ken's parents put it this way: "In any situation when someone is going to get the short end of the stick – you be the one to get the short end of the stick."

This powerful statement became the way Ken would live his life, always "preferring" others. It is important to him that focus, recognition, and awards be placed on others, not him. I asked him how that made him feel. He replied, "It makes me feel like a grown man." Meekness, humbleness, and calmness all demonstrate strength!

As we continued to talk, he shared more wisdom he learned from his family. He said, "We are the sum total of everything we have experienced." In addressing stressful or difficult times, he continued, "All things will look different in the morning."

Ken would never say it, but he is an important person in our community. He is the force behind the scenes that makes things happen. As part of his job, he is the stage contact for performers. He has met many famous people including Rhonda Vincent, Sam Bush, the Isaacs, Ricky Skaggs, the Osborne Brothers, Doc Watson, Donna Fargo, and the Lonesome River Band, to name a few. He holds an especially important position in the Arts community.

For all the famous people he has met, and because of the important position he holds, it would be easy for Ken to be egotistical or arrogant, but he is the opposite.

Outwardly, he portrays the spirit of a lamb, but inwardly, he is one of the strongest men in our community. He is meek, humble, and always calm. His good DNA and the environmental influences of his saintly parents and his godly grandfather come together to make him a great man.

It is important to understand that meekness provides the strength necessary for control. Control allows us to manage our emotions. We can allow the LIGHT of positive influencers to lead us to a courageous place.

Ken is a local hero, a man of courage, and a positive influence. Since the second publication of this book, Ken has retired from The Surry Arts Council.

Our small town is filled with heroes.

Calvin B. Vaughn, Jr.

Charity...Miss Angel

She heard the big people whispering.

The five-year-old could see that her best friend's skin was pale. Her little playmate was often sick with a fever, and she had a cough that would not go away.

As they played, Carolyn would easily bruise, sometimes bleed, and have trouble breathing. What Angela could not see was that her best chum had too many white blood cells in her lungs, causing an enlarged spleen, damaged liver, and swollen lymph nodes. Her small friend had childhood leukemia - cancer of the bone marrow.

The innocent children, with typical vocabularies, did not know, nor did they understand the "C" word. In their normal linguistic development, they grasped simple concepts like today, tomorrow, or yesterday. They knew seasons and they could recognize some words by sight, but the meaning of disease and death would come much too early for the harmless tots.

The frail friend became weaker. Angela's compassion grew stronger. With the tenderness of a child, she wanted to do something for her sick friend. She wanted her to be able to buy toys and things she wanted.

She had a simple idea. Together, with another friend, and her family, she set up a lemonade stand, along with sweets. The savory smell of freshly baked cookies slowly flooded the nostrils of the girls as they gently positioned each one on the table. The simple, yet notable, venture was a mountainous triumph. They gathered treasured coins and gave them to Carolyn, their ailing friend. Now, she could buy whatever toy she wanted.

As the toy collection grew, the strong treatments did too. The hair of the weakened child with cancer began to fall out. Angela's mom crocheted hats for her. She made each one a different color so she would have one for each outfit.

The little girl with lots of hats never saw her sixth birthday, but she did see charity through her friend's act of love.

As Angela Noflo began to understand the full meaning of cancer and death, she also began to learn and comprehend a more powerful word - charity. A word that would be ever-growing in her heart and shape her destiny. Like a constant stream, more ideas of how to respond to a need with love continued to flow. Throughout her life, the stream continued to widen. Today, a river of love flows.

Although the Noflo family was extremely poor, Angela remembers, heartfelt generosity sprinkled in her dad's daily prayers. Each night, at the dinner table, either during the prayer or immediately after, her little ears heard his solemn expression, "If you give from your heart, you'll get back twice fold."

With open ears and a receptive heart, the tiny redhead, with insight beyond her years, thoughtfully asked her dad, "What does that mean?" With a soft, yet deep conviction, he responded in love, "God hears everything you say and do as long as you do it from your heart."

She pondered her dad's words. She soaked the profound wisdom into her childlike spirit shaping her heart of love. The foundation for her life's purpose was being laid.

After experiencing the death of her young friend, her childhood was less dramatic. She grew up in Long Island, New York. She spent her youthful years like most young girls, except she was watching her dad's slow progression of declining health.

An ailing father had become a normal part of life. He had been sick for as long as she could remember. She developed a youthful level of concern, as she watched him survive three open-heart surgeries.

Twenty-one years after her friend's death, Angela had

an experience that cemented her life's direction and molded her into the generous woman she is today. She was nine months pregnant with her first child when the transformative event happened. Sharing the cathartic crisis, she declared. "This struggle made me who I am today." The life-changing episode was like no other.

Mr. Noflo was excited to be a first-time grandfather. With joy, he scampered off to do some shopping for his daughter's shower. He knew he was moving quickly, so he ignored the shortness of breath. But then, the uncomfortable pressure began to squeeze like someone was tightening a belt around his chest. His arm tingled as he suddenly felt dizzy – in an instant – CRACK!

As he pummeled to the ground his head struck the pavement like a heavy stone rolling from a mountain rockslide. All went dark. Total silence. He lay, unaided, and unconscious for 15 minutes. After finally being rescued, the paramedics recorded on his medical sheet, "Head trauma, searching for brain activity."

The emergency room doctor read the report. Connecting the patient to a bundle of wires he was probing for a response. Life-detecting machines glowed and beeped confirming the initial assessment.

The phone rang, announcing the moment her life would change forever. As quickly as a mother-to-be at full term can move, she rushed to the hospital. She had always been remarkably close to her dad. Her emotions were gushing faster than her body could move.

Arriving at the hospital and shuffling to the waiting room, she heard the doctor's piercing report. He is in a comma, there is no brain activity. For a moment, her world stopped. Numbness began to take over her body. She and her mother hugged.

For the next few hours, they sat, often in silence. The date burned an imprint onto her memory.

The next couple of days were spent in the hospital. After

two days without hopeful progress, the expectant mother was encouraged to go home for much-needed rest.

She went home, fretting over her father and wrestling for rest, as her body was preparing for the delivery. Fighting the uncomfortable fatigue, she fell asleep.

The phone rang, once again, declaring a time of transformation. She looked at the clock, it was 2:00 am. With dread and a low voice, " She muttered, "Hel----lo?" In a calm, but sure voice the woman said, "Your dad is not looking good, and I just wanted to tell you that you and your mom need to come back to the hospital in the morning."

Assured, she could wait a few hours, she lay back down to get a little rest before getting her mom and heading back to the hospital. Her strength was drained, and she fell asleep quickly. Her eyes opened wide - someone had touched her. With a tinge of fear, a slice of worry, and a whole lot pregnant she turned her eyes toward the touch.

She saw a man. Closing her eyes tight and opening them again, she quickly thought. "Am I dreaming?"

She was rubbing her eyes when the phone shouted for attention. The man disappeared. It was 3:05 pm. She whispered to herself. "I must be hallucinating." Again, picking up the dreadful telephonic messenger, she answered as a woman awakened out of sleep. She heard the same assuring voice with a hint of excitement, "We need you now, your dad is off life support and breathing on his own."

Angela was stunned!

Eighty-five minutes later, the familiar halls echoed in silence as she and her mom made their way to the nurse's station. The kind woman in white escorted them into the room, and she encouraged them, "Talk to him. I think he can hear you." Smiling, she turns and leaves the room.

Holding his arm and patting his hand, the pregnant daughter calls out, "Daddy." No response. With a stronger voice, she repeats, "Daddy, Daddy, Daddy, can you hear me?" The cycle is repeated in rhythm like the second hand on a watch. Her watermelon belly forced her to adjust her position on the side of the bed. Fretfully demanding she expelled, "Squeeze my hand...nod...make a move!"

Her voice grew loud, "Daddy can you hear me?" Silence held the room hostage. Nothing. The silence grew louder only to be muffled by the continuous beeping of the life-giving machines.

Rehearsing the events of the night, she recalls the touch, the man that disappeared, and the call that relayed the sudden improvement of her dad, all created false hope. She grappled with understanding.

Again, and again, in desperation, she cried out to her dad! Adding a hint of anger, she continued, "Why did you call me down here if you are not going to talk to me."

After a long time, through tearful swollen eyes, she saw him turn his head. He faced her. A rivulet oozed down his moistened cheek. With expectancy, she leaned forward, breathlessly waiting for him to speak. There was no sound. His mouth never moved. As she continued to glare, her emotions raced like cars on a superhighway; she did not understand. Anger seeped, leaking from her mixed feelings.

It would be several days before she understood the language of tears.

The nurse returned and saw her frustration, and with confidence, she spoke, "Oh, I think he can hear you, even if he is not responding."

After a few hours, her pregnancy could not be ignored, she curtly said, "I have to go home, and get some rest." Misty-eyed, she left the room. Tears rolled down her cheeks as she neared the elevator. Hurt, pain, and anger dripped from her wet face. Wiping her tears, she entered the cage.

As the door closed, it felt like a prison, then it moved. She turned to avoid facing the man in the back. After a moment, the stranger behind her spoke with a caring voice,

"Why are you crying, why are you bitter, don't be bitter." He continued with angelic calmness, "Your dad is at peace."

Frozen in consciousness, she did not move, her face fixed on the door. The bell dings as the elevator arrives at the bottom floor. She felt it was time to turn and see the gentleman that offered the peaceful words. She slowly turned. He was gone! There was no one there.

She trembled as she walked to her car. By the time she was in the car, she was shaking. Her hands were jerking like a leaf on a windy day. The drive was difficult, but she finally arrived home.

In familiar surroundings, she became settled. Trying to put it all together, she pondered, "This is the most interesting night I have ever experienced." The feelings and thoughts of that night created the lowest point of her life.

She had only been at home a couple of hours when the news arrived, dad was back on the ventilator. In two days, he would pass. Angela and the family grieved. Friends and family gathered for support.

A few days after the funeral, she was cleaning out old papers of her dad's. She found a letter; she sat down and began to read.

To my little angel,

There is nothing I want more than for you to be a wonderful mom. Always know that I am with you - always. Remember, do everything from the heart, just like you were taught. You are the chosen one.

Love, your dad

It became clear. The strange night had profound meaning. With an understanding that grew, she believed that dad had heard her. She reflected. His turning head, his eyes fixed on her, he spoke with tears, he was saying goodbye.

She had wanted more, she had wanted something different, but this unsettling experience had brought peace. Later she acknowledged, the most difficult night of her life turned into the perfect morning.

As I sat at a table in her bakery, while she shared her story, she admitted. "This was the freakiest thing that ever happened in my life." Mystified, she continued, "I don't know why I witnessed such an unusual thing." With confidence, she concluded, "I know I am called to charity."

Absorbing what I heard, I could clearly see. As if a blinding curtain had been opened; I too understood. The influence of a father's Godly prayer, the receptivity of a child's tender heart, the compassion born through suffering, and the acceptance of being chosen explained the metamorphosis. No longer did I wonder why she is called *Miss Angel*.

In 2005, Miss Angel, her husband Randy Shur, and two children moved to Mount Airy, North Carolina. Their eldest adult daughter followed a few years later. The family lives on a 65-acre farm in the Pine Ridge area, nine miles west of Mount Airy. The farm brims with activity providing a busy schedule with pick-your-own fruit and weekend events for the whole family. (see Appendix III Beyond MAin...Miss Angel's Farm)

She opened a bakery, located in the heart of downtown, called *Miss Angels Heavenly Pies*. The bakery has been given national and state awards along with outstanding reviews. The magazine *Taste of Home* called it "the best bakery in North Carolina, and *Our State* magazine called it "a slice of heaven". (see Appendix II More on MAin...Bakeries and Candy Stores)

Each day at the bakery, Miss Angel demonstrates love. Any unsold baked goods are distributed among the food banks, charities, and shelters located in the area to help feed our homeless and others in need. Often, sweets and many times whole meals are specifically prepared fresh for someone in need. The Shur family has supported more than 25 agencies' fundraising events, plus multiple churches have benefited from their giving. The bakery has become a house of charity.

In September 2019, Miss Angel launched *"Touched by Miss Angel Charitable Trust,"* a private, non-profit foundation, serving Alzheimer's patients from all over Surry County, and their families, friends, and caregivers.

During the 2020 Covid-19 pandemic, her charitable endeavors reached frontline workers and provided home-cooked meals. She rallied the community to write cards for isolated seniors in facilities. She gave a cupcake to each older adult getting a card.

Over a lifetime of giving, her heart for charity increased with keen perception. One of the many heartwarming examples is the touching story of a mom and child. A ten-year-old child, along with her mom came into the bakery. After looking at the huge display of goodies, the child, while whispering to her mom, opened a tiny torn coin purse.

Unnoticed, in the background, Miss Angel sensed the situation and assessed the need. Meticulously, the mother began counting each coin. Gingerly, with the softness of a lamb, the mom mumbled, "It's my daughter's birthday, what can I get for $2.00?"

In a New York minute, the bakery owner sparkled with a response, "Wow, you are in luck, I've got a special on today that you will love." Standing nearby, her son and daughter were listening. Words of communication from their mom were not needed. They knew the drill. Many times, they had seen the hands and feet of love.

Like a perfectly running machine, they went to work. The caring son wheeled around, headed toward the back, and in a flash returned with a cone mounted with homemade ice cream. Again, with no spoken words, her tender-hearted daughter headed toward the kitchen and began to create a special birthday tray filled with goodies.

In angelic harmony, Miss Angel selected a huge cookie sandwich with homemade filling – nothing but the best, the famous chocolate chip banjo (a house specialty). Like a rare gem, she placed it gently in a beautifully decorated box and handed it to the birthday girl.

The little girl's eyes twinkled like stars and gleamed like the sun. The mother smiled with overwhelming relief.

Like any family, during the years, the Shurs have overcome life's challenges. Currently, her husband has an incurable rheumatoid disease-causing chronic discomfort. The health issue requires ongoing expensive treatments, but that has not slowed him or her down in their work or their acts of charity.

Some have asked, "How do you do it?" She responded. "This is who I am, you are not going to change my red hair

and challenging times are not going to change who I am." She further shared, "More important to me than buying new clothes or dinner, I can feed children in need or someone hungry."

Through her own childhood experience, she learned to love and the power of influence that can mold a child. To her children, with passion, she shared with them these words, "Make me proud, when I am up there, do good things, even if you don't keep the store open. When you love, you love."

Years ago, few people realized, a little girl, a small act of charity, and a lemonade stand would lead to a purpose-filled life. The stand is long *Miss Angel and Her Husband* stream, love grew, expandin charity. Destiny fulfilled. Although she is not originally from our small town, she and her family portray all that is good about small-town America.

Each of us is born to destiny. Discovering yours provides purpose and allows you to live love out loud.

Charity never fails in our small town.

Community...James Massey

"I like the idea of small-town America." He revealed. "It reminds me of the idyllic life of Mayberry."

It was the second time he had visited our town with a population of 10,000. It was the first time he lodged at the baronial inn filled with works of art. Before settling comfortably on the wicker chair adorning the front porch, he and I had enjoyed a delectable meal prepared by culinary artist and co-owner of the Vermeer Bed and Breakfast. Relaxed and cozy, he continued. (see Appendix III Beyond MAin...Bed & Breakfast)

Recalling an age of innocence, he remembered the charm of a community where people know and care about each other. "People are too busy; they don't take the time to care." He spoke with experience. "A small town provides an easier opportunity for a real sense of community."

He reminisced further, describing what he called an age of innocence. Much like the time portrayed through the 1960s popular show that helped put our small town on the map. Some say it was happier times when families spent time together and the community functioned as a village. He fondly spoke about meaningful and compassionate interactions. As he shared with calm conviction, it was peaceful. I felt like the world paused. I knew I was going to enjoy my conversation with James Massey.

He grew up in the South and attended the University of Georgia for his undergraduate degree and he studied at Shippensburg University for his MBA.

As a patriot from a military family, he served as an officer in the United States Army. His military service included time in the National Guard and the U.S. Army Reserve. During his career, he was on staff at the Army War College in Carlisle, Pennsylvania where he developed an appreciation for education. The position provided a path to become a graduate of the Defense Information School and the Command and General Staff College. He retired after twenty-two years of service.

His education and military experience opened the door for a second career at the Pennsylvania Department of Education, where he was the State Administrator for the Child Care Food Program and the Summer Food Service Program.

Much of his military service and most of his civilian service was spent in metropolitan areas. He became familiar with the challenges of the inner city. He saw firsthand the results of the breakdown of family and community.

During his service to the country, his compassion and love for people grew. After meeting the love of his life, Madelyn, he gained a life partner who shared his love for social service.

She was born and raised in Philadelphia. She graduated as valedictorian of her class and was offered a full scholarship to the University of Pennsylvania. After much thought, and a desire to broaden her horizons, she refused it and chose to go outside of the city and attend Dickinson College.

She returned to her hometown to study at Drexel University for graduate school. She became an academic librarian and faculty member at Dickinson College where she taught for twenty-two years. Her profession in education included time at Penn State University, and Harrisburg Area Community College.

Together, they built a life filled with satisfaction and success. Much of their contentment grew from community and caring.

The Masseys have always placed importance on continuing one's education to become a well-rounded individual who appreciates the arts, literature, music, nature, and athletics. They both saw how a lack of community support in the inner city was hindering young people from education. They decided to make a difference.

Moved with benevolence, they started The James and Madelyn Massey Scholarship for Education. They hoped that young people would experience something positive. They felt the small-town college experience away from the ills of the inner city would result in building a better community.

Their generosity expanded to support two other scholarship programs. One at the University of Georgia for a deserving member of a 4-H Club and one for a deserving student in Sierra Leon. The out-of-state, and international support demonstrated their desire to serve and their view that humankind is one community.

Throughout their life, they exhibited community service, which eventually led Jim to pursue a political career. As his initial campaign success was announced, Madelyn's health concerns were discovered.

She was diagnosed with breast cancer that would spread. Things changed. Declining health became the journey, yet they experienced the riches of community and family. He warmly remembers all the support during their time of struggle.

She was strong and Jim was her support until the end. He drew strength from friends, family, and community. In the fall of 2019, he became a widower. Now, more than ever, he valued community.

Caring is found in community. Close relationships are natural in the simple living of a small town, and the closeness can make it easier to show how people care about each other.

He described his experience in making connections. "I travel across this country, and too many times I see that the sense of community is dropped. I wave at people, and they are too busy to notice. I care. I love people regardless of how well-known they are or how little they are known. I see all people the same."

Connective caring can be easier in a small town, however, in a large city, you can have a small-town heart. During the 2020 pandemic, Jim modeled caring to those he had worked with. He contacted each member of the department of education, from the janitor to the director, and encouraged them. With sincerity and a compassionate heart, to the essential frontline workers, he gave an uplifting message. To each one, he said. "Very often you are forgotten, but you are the ones that make a difference – you matter. You are positive examples that make a big difference."

During the pandemic, he searched for something positive, and he saw encouraging signs. "One blessing of the pandemic is that people seem to be getting back to being friendly, I notice more people caring for their neighbor." He noted that in past snowstorms common to his area, people cared, but it was over in two days. Now, seven months to a year after the crisis of the worldwide virus – people are still caring.

With insight, he stated, "We are a world village, you can be in Charlotte today and Hong Kong tomorrow. The smallness of the world makes community more important." He continued. "We have got to get the sense of family and community back." It is a simple gesture to wave, but the simple act may be the first step in connecting to community.

People in our small town continue to wave at each other, even strangers. Try it, you might connect to someone on Main Street.

A veteran in the July Parade, honoring all veterans

Compassion...Amy Heath

"Sta – iiiiiink - eeee – Sta – iiiiiiink - eee – stinky, stinky, stinky!" Echoed the tonal rhythmic pattern of the first grader with ginger hair and spotted freckles. The young boy, along with his classmates, caught the stench of the unpleasant odor reeking from the little girl.

Her clothes were soiled, faded, and wrinkled. The other little boys joined in to sing the made-up melody, and the little girls snickered. The teacher scolded the class. Giggling, they all stopped.

Not understanding her feelings, with empathy, and a questioning frown, Amy looked at the little one with the foul smell. The dirty tangled hair of the girl flowed gently, covering her face, and masking the hurt. Amy felt something that guided the rest of her life. At the end of the school day, at home with her mom, she described the event.

Her mom taught a lesson that would be repeated many times. With a compassionate and loving voice, she said, "Be good to everyone, but especially, be nice to stinkers who don't have good clothes."

The next heart-changing lesson came after Archie moved next door. The cute little seven-year-old was full of life, just like any other little boy, but he could not hear or speak. Her mother used this opportunity to instill another lesson of compassion, but this time with action. Mom bought a set of teaching cards for her daughter to learn how to communicate in sign language.

If she learned sign language, the deaf boy would not have to play alone. Her mother said, "You have to learn to be good to everybody, even people with special needs." This lesson was easy for her to grasp, no one had taught her to be unkind, or judgmental.

Since the age of two, Amy Heath had started to show

signs of genuine empathy. On her journey to becoming a caring and compassionate woman, her mother's wisdom was a guide.

Someone else, unexpectantly, contributed to her maturing compassion, Captain Kangaroo. The children's television series, starring the Captain, aired from 1966 to 1984. It was a popular program. Most of the neighborhood kids were faithful viewers.

Captain Kangaroo promoted the Muscular Dystrophy Association (MDA). The MDA is a nonprofit health agency dedicated to curing muscular dystrophy, and related diseases by funding worldwide research.

Images of kids in wheelchairs were shown during the MDA promotion. She had never seen a kid in a wheelchair. Her eyes froze on the metal, trying to process the seated child's limitations. The feelings that moved her to be kind to the "stinky" little girl coursed through her young soul.

With a flash, the spokesperson appealed to help "Jerry's Kids". Next, the black and white tv screen filled with kids in a carnival atmosphere, with lots of kids, laughing, playing, and running.

The kind face of the suited man from the MDA popped on the screen again. His face engulfed the entire 21 inches of the glass box. With thrilling words and excitement in his voice, he announced, "You can host a Backyard Carnival, you can help 'Jerry's Kids'".

Naturally, Amy's tender heart moved with compassion, prompting her to order the kit. It included everything a kid needed to host a carnival. The homemade games were entertaining and full of merriment, especially the fortune-teller booth. The carnival helped raise money for the cause while teaching valuable lessons of compassion. Amy continued to journey on the path of compassion.

In Junior High, Rita was often alone. She was shunned, and few people understood epilepsy during that time. The disorder caused unusual sensations that sometimes resulted in the loss of awareness and the loss of friends. She was the next recipient of Amy's growing compassion.

The central nervous system disorder provoked Rita's seizures and occasionally led to wetting herself. During these episodes, Amy stayed with her in the sick room, until fresh clothes were delivered.

Amy developed the ability to identify pain in others. She looked beyond the exterior and could see a wounded heart. Her mother was proud of the way her daughter was becoming a kind woman, she said, "Anyone would be lucky to have you as a friend."

Yet, she knew pain. Her wounds made it easy to see and feel what others felt. Hurt had been an early and constant companion. Her dad's drinking problem created havoc in the home. Her earliest memories are going to Al-Anon (a support group for loved ones of alcoholics).

The little girl tried to hide from the trauma of alcoholism; however, her eyes and ears saw and heard the chaos. As a child, she was defenseless against the unpredictability of the alcoholic's impulses and desires.

Many times, she faced the darkness alone. She could not have friends at the house, for fear, they would be traumatized. Barely reaching the waist of her daddy, she often came out from hiding, trying to calm him down and hide the liquid fire, the source of destruction.

His ability to function progressively got worse. Before she was a teenager, she experienced a lot of inner pain alone. Sometimes it felt like her loving mother was the only one trying to help relieve the difficulties of being raised in the home of an alcoholic.

The teen who was an only child became a sister. Now, there was another little girl who could be harmed by the effects of a parent's hard drinking. She and her mom wanted to shelter the newborn baby from the devastation. When dad went on a binge, the mom would take the little one and escape to a safer place in West Virginia.

Frequently, they would be gone for weeks. In their absence, Amy went to school, worked, cared for the home, and took care of dad. Mom and sis returned when he sobered up.

He had a pattern. He worked for two or three months, made a lot of money, got liquored up, and went on a bender to gamble or drink the money away. He would come home soused with 100 bills, or on the other extreme, come home after squandering the money on a camper, boat, go-cart, or something else that took the place of basic needs.

He was a gambler. In poker games, he won big, and he lost big. Losing the house in a poker game became a cycle, that their uncle would rescue them from time and time again. In good times, the family had their needs met and often they had nice things. But other times, things were tight because of all the gambling and the wasteful spending.

More times than she wants to recount, she had to go to a bootlegger's house, to a gambling room, or to a bar to rescue her dad. At the age of sixteen, she drove him out of state, two hours away, to a rehab facility. It did not last. He returned home by the time she did. This too became a cycle.

Most of her teen years were given to caregiving for a drunken dad. She always had a soft place in her heart for him, you could even say she had compassion for the wretched and ravaged life he lived.

In high school, teachers connected with her, observing her kind spirit and compassionate heart. They also detected her homelife challenges. They took her under their wings.

A school trip to Carowinds (an NC theme park) was scheduled. Dad was on a binge. There was no money for extras. Ms. Spainhour and Ms. Albright paid the fee for her to go. With warm emotions, Amy said, "That meant so much to me."

Another teacher, Ms. Bailey, embraced her with a maternal instinct and pushed her to academic and vocational success. She encouraged her to participate in the

Distributive Education Club (DECA).

DECA's mission is to prepare emerging leaders and entrepreneurs. Representing the club, she won several awards, once even going to Washington DC to receive recognition. To this day, she and Ms. Baily remain close. Amy is appreciative of the teachers who influenced, nurtured, and supported her.

Two years after graduation, she married. Following the path that adult children of alcoholics take, she experienced an unhealthy relationship for 28 years. Her mother had an alcoholic father, and an alcoholic husband and through example, she learned to live in chaos. She was verbally and physically abused. A cycle of separating and returning repeatedly. Her abuser always convinced her to return. It took years, but eventually, he let go, and she did too.

Living in the shadow of a troubled childhood and the darkness of an abusive marriage, she found relief through work. Emerged in the toil of a local textile mill, she became a star employee. From an entry-level position, she advanced to supervise the embroidery department. With her talent, an idea, or a picture, she could design anything.

She had a keen ability for artistic development. Her craft of embroidery design received recognition. National magazines highlighted her work. Her embroidery creations received awards from international companies. One of her greatest honors was being asked to design the embroidered logo for the Marine Helicopter Squadron One. The squadron is responsible for the transportation of the president of the United States and other heads of state. The secret service member who worked with her during the process became a good friend.

She attracts friends easily. Most people enjoy her honesty and bubbly personality. Many have experienced her authentic care and true compassion. Many become lifelong friends.

Carolyn, one of her lifelong friends, developed cancer.

Amy became her constant companion. She walked with her on the journey, attending doctor's appointments and raising money for her medical bills. In the obituary, she was listed as a sister and sat with the family during the funeral.

Another friend, Pat Littleton, developed a close relationship with her at work. When the textile mill followed the bloodletting to Mexico, they became business partners.

Chaos erupted, in the mill, the day the plant announced its closing. A few cried some cursed, and others wandered around as a man dazed from a hard blow. When Amy got the news, without hesitation, she headed to Pat's office. The strong and resilient woman marched in with grit, determination, and hope. They discussed what was happening and in no time, they had a plan.

On a prayer and $1000, the business was launched. **Mayberry Embroidery** (a customized clothing embroidery business) is located on Main Street. What some thought was impossible, especially without knowledge of being small business owners, they became successful businesswomen.

A setback occurred with the recession of 2008. Once again, the survivor survived. Her compassion survived as well.

During her busy adult years, she remained a caregiver. Amy, her mom, and her sister nurtured their dad during his final illness. He lingered for about one year. At the same time as her dad's languishing health, her mother's health began to weaken. During the time of her mom's debilitating health, the sisters were the caretakers. After their dad's death, their mom would live three more years. Although the caretaking

Amy Heath

her

need to care for others did not.

On a sunny Sunday morning, Amy had an encounter that opened a fresh opportunity to share compassion. She met Sam and his family at church. The developmentally disabled 30-year-old lived by himself in public housing. For much of his life, his sisters had taken care of his basic needs, but they were limited in their ability to help him to engage socially.

From a child, Amy had connected with the marginalized. Her connection to Sam was natural. Remembering the lesson from her mom, (and little Archie), she was drawn to him. Their friendship was immediate and grew. Everyone liked him, she did too. She helped him get involved in community events.

Soon after meeting him, she discovered Special Olympics and became a volunteer. She loved it. All in with both feet, she started coaching basketball and bowling. It was not long before she had Sam sign up as an athlete. He loved it. Together, they went to sports activities, including state competitions. They enjoyed the competitions in bowling at the Mount Airy Bowling Lanes. The sports venue is a strong supporter of the Special Olympics. (see Appendix III Beyond MAin...Sports and Game Venues)

Developing a circle of friends, Sam began to blossom. Fondly remembering, Amy reminisced, "We had the best time playing games, attending events, and making new friends." The social engagement led him to become more independent. She assisted in helping him upgrade his living situation. When he moved, he thought he had a mansion. Today, he is doing good and living independently. They remain great friends.

During that same time, her aunt by marriage became ill and needed help. The aunt had not been nice to Amy or the family, but Amy's compassion looked through the crusty façade of flesh and saw a need. For the next ten years, she would serve as her caregiver.

She never stopped being concerned about others, even when she went through her own health scare with a melanoma diagnosis.

Her future became brighter when she met Michael. He was instrumental in supporting Amy in breaking from the past. He demonstrated how a lady is supposed to be treated. He spoke to her words of affirmation that encouraged and built her up. In the beginning, it was challenging to accept because of the past, filled with years of put-downs. After months of consistent positive support, she began to feel like a princess. Lovingly she declared "He was brought into my life to help me get to where I am today. I am blessed to have him in my life."

They dated for a few years and then they became remarkably close. The friendship developed into a healthy relationship. Today, they are best friends.

Through the long journey to wholeness, Amy discovered her value and emerged from the dark past of a troubled childhood. She climbed out of an abusive marriage. She broke the strangling connection to the past. And she built healthy relationships.

It took years of counseling, self-improvement, strength, perseverance, and determination, but she is in a better place. Now, her focus is on self-wellness, making decisions that support her own total health. She continues to learn about codependency, boundaries, and balance. Healing continues, and so does compassion.

Over time, Amy has learned valuable lessons. For example, stepping in to "fix" the problem by doing all the work creates more concerns. It robs the wounded person of the opportunity to learn to advocate for themselves. The best way to nurture a hurting person is to first nurture your own pain. Accepting that truth, along with knowing you cannot fix it all, gives one more time to focus on fixing yourself. She, also learned people must be ready to make positive change, you cannot do it for them, and you can only support the decision they make.

A recent experience provides an example of her mature compassion. A tall slender lady with long black hair came into the store. Carrying a suitcase, she looked a little ragged. Amy perceived she was homeless, probably broken and in need. She got to know her and helped her.

She offered to assist her in getting housing. Choices were offered, allowing the woman to make her own decisions. Then Amy let go. She knew the compassion she felt with the offer to help was enough - now it was up to the down and out to help herself, develop a plan and change her situation.

As I reviewed Amy's life, I saw a constant thread woven throughout her journey. When I told her, I thought she had a lot of compassion, she shrilled with an endearing country twang, "I would do 'anythang' I could for everybody as much as I can for all I can." She further stated, "I'll stand with you, beside you, and go through it with you." Through it all, she declared, "I am very blessed."

Today, the happy, healthy, and successful businesswoman is proud of herself, and she is proud of her daughter (a healthcare professional) and grandchildren.

Growing up in a small town you often see compassionate kindness performed by people and to people you know. Brushing shoulders with them, regularly, makes it easier to live the golden rule.

Our small town is clothed with compassion, thanks to people like Amy.

1-888-4AL-ANON 1-888-425-2666

Connected...Jennie Lowry

Little by little she was fading, like an old dress, unrecognizable, as if it had been washed too many times. If you did not know her, you could have a conversation as if nothing was muddled. But she had Alzheimer's.

The same lyrics kept ringing. The repetition could be tiresome, sometimes a little irritating, and other times cutely comical. Yet, the song like a broken record brought closeness, connecting granddaughter and grandma each time.

No doubt, during her long life, she had sung the song 1000 times.

Again, they continued.

Swing low, sweet chariot
Coming for to carry me home
Swing low sweet chariot
Coming for to carry me home

The dreaded disease of Alzheimer's causes faces to be less familiar and meaningful conversations to be less frequent. Yet, in a musical moment, yesteryear's familiar hymn awakes awareness.

Research shows music connects to those with Alzheimer's and dementia when nothing else can. It is powerful how music flows into the subconscious level. Like a key, it unlocks a door into the brain, opening fresh familiarity. It is a powerful universal melody.

For most of her life, Jennie Lowry understood the power of music. Convincingly, she said, "Music is the connective tissue to life." For that reason, and a million more, she has always loved music. She further explained, "It does not matter what you do for a living, or what clothes you wear. It does not matter the church you attend or the beliefs you have, all people are the same. Everyone is connected through music." The connection is amazing.

Childhood connections influenced her love for music. Jam sessions, church singings, and most of all, her paternal grandmother's love for "ole time music." Her grandmother played the guitar and piano. Music was always a part of family gatherings. During those times, she taught Jennie how to harmonize.

Jennie's first instrument was a paisley pink guitar. The twelve-year-old's great timing and ear for music were developed by playing back up with her dad and traveling locally with her talented uncle, Boyd McKinney.

Full of talent, in junior high, she played fiddle in the orchestra. With an impressive ability, she sang harmony in the show choir. Expanding her gift, she began to play the flute, claw hammer banjo, ukulele, and recently the piano. She loves all types of music, but her favorite styles areold-timee traditional bluegrass or classics.

According to Jennie, the connection to family, friends, and community through music has led her to a happier and more fulfilled life.

"I have always noticed the power of music to connect people, and recently, I understood how." She explained. "For example, if you go to a fiddler's convention, you may not be playing, but you are participating – you feel a part of the music."

With music, individuals become a symphony of people. The musician on stage, the singer with the mic, the sound guy, the concession worker, the parking attendant, and the audience, everyone feels a part of the music. Toes tap, hands clap, some dance, and others just bob their head to the beat. But everyone is connected.

Each Saturday morning, Jennie connects with audiences across America. She hosts the Merry-Go-Round at the Earl Theatre. It is the second oldest ongoing live radio show in the nation behind the Grand Ole Opry. The Women in Surry County Old-Time Music Exhibit, located in the theatre, honors her as a gifted musician and recognizes her distinction of being the first female host of the weekly historical show. People from all over the nation and local music lovers visit the on-air bluegrass experience.

Round Peak, a small community nestled in the southern Appalachian Mountains, about 10 miles west of Mount Airy, is the hollow where this area's unique tradition of fiddle and banjo music was discovered. Through jam sessions, the Round Peak bluegrass style has connected community for generations. (see Appendix III Beyond MAin...Jam Sessions)

Each year, the Mount Airy Old-Time Fiddler's Convention at the Veteran's Park connects 1000s of local, national, and international musicians and fans. Crowds start flowing to the convention the week before the event, and many stay after the convention. Campsites fill quickly. There is dancing, singing, education, and entertainment for the whole family. Jam sessions breakout, allowing everyone to feel they are a part. (see Appendix III Beyond MAin...Veteran's Park and Beyond MAin...Old-Time Fiddler's Convention)

She loves her musical heritage, but she values more, her present-day connection to people. "I think a huge benefit of living in a small town is the ease of connecting with others. In a large city, you get lost in the shuffle of a busy life."

Chasing a dream, like so many, her musical family moved to the capital of country music when she was a toddler. Growing up in Nashville, the feelings of being disconnected became familiar. She felt invisible.

While in the Music City, her family found success. Her mom, a talented performer, had a lot of bookings. Her dad became well-known in the country music scene. For years, he played with the Donna Fargo band. He was the band leader and a tour bus driver. After the country music star stopped touring, and because of his connections, he was able to play 'fill-in gigs' for other country artists. (see Appendix III Beyond MAin...Donna Fargo and Beyond MAin...Jimmy

Lowry)

Living over 400 miles from their hometown, the Lowry family remained connected to friends and family. As a young girl, she remembers being in Mount Airy almost every holiday. Often, summers were spent with her grandparents.

The family's connection to their roots made it easy to move back when the paternal grandfather became ill and needed assistance. The return for her was like making a 180-degree turn. She recalls some aspects of the bigger city were enjoyable but, in her hometown, she treasured community.

Her parents loved reconnecting with former friends. They began to play with local bands, and musicians they knew before touring the country music world. The reunion amplified good times and renewed relationships.

Jennie noted, "If I were not in a "small community" like this one, the connection to others would not be possible." In her experience, even the process of connecting with persons who move into our small town is effortless and beneficial. She has found it easy to connect with tourists as well. Furthermore, she stated, "In a small town, making friends is uncomplicated.

"In a charming little town, like Mount Airy, it is easy to connect and build relationships. For example, often, you are seated by familiar faces in a local café, or you know the names of those near you at a concert. By seeing your neighbors more frequently, you are presented with more opportunities to grow friendships.

"Compared to a larger city, in a smaller town, there is accountability, which makes you a more responsible citizen." She added, "Being responsible through accountability is a benefit of living in a place where most people know your name." Speaking with experience, she disclosed, "If you do something bad in a big city, your family might not know about it. But, here in a small town, you are kept in check."

It is not a bad thing. It helps you be more conscious about how your words or actions affect yourself and other people, enabling better decision-making skills. To show you what I mean, if you treat the person you pass on the street with disrespect, you may very well see them that afternoon at the local grocery checkout counter. On Monday, if you get angry with the customer service representative at City Hall, on Sunday, you might find yourself looking across the church and seeing them seated on the other side. The older gentleman in the parking lot, you were kind to, and allowed to go in front of you, might be the same man to greet you with kindness at the local hardware store.

A little town seeds an opportunity for connection. Connection waters responsibility. Responsibility grows accountability.

"I like people and I love people in this community." She fondly stated. "The community teaches me a lot, and I want to be a servant to the community.

"We are all walking the same few blocks. There is something comforting about walking down the street and knowing the people you meet," she cozily noted. It allows relationships to grow, friendships to develop, and true connections to happen.

The Lowrys are a close-knit family. Usually, the mom, the three talented children, and their grandmother are together. The dad is always close by.

The homeschooled kids join the adults in multiple community events held at the Regional Museum, the Arts Council, school bands, and city-wide activities. Most local festivals benefit from the musical talents of the whole family. Their mom believes their music is a wonderful way to build community connection. Faith is important to the family, as well, they play and sing in the church band. (see Appendix II More on MAin...Festivals)

She sees opportunities all around Mount Airy that make

it easy for anyone to connect through music. One example is the free weekly music and dance lessons for youth offered through the Surry Arts Council. With enthusiasm, she added, "You can go to free jams, free dance lessons, or join a community choir at no cost. Attend live performances, enjoy the music, or learn an instrument from one of the many local teachers. It all makes you musical." Music helps you connect, whether you are listening, playing, or singing.

She believes there is music within everyone and that you can find the inner music at any age. She tells everyone, you do not have to play professionally, you can play as a hobby or for fun. Try different things. Sing, dance, or just pat your foot. "It should all be for enjoyment."

She understands some people self-proclaim that they are not musical. Jennie responds, "Oh, but yes you are, everyone is musical. There is a melody within each of us."

Affirming her belief, she confessed. "I love all music, we limit ourselves, by not being open to music. You should go hear music whatever type you like. The two most important things about music are: 1. Make it fun. 2. Pass down traditional music to the next generation."

One of our local radio stations, WPAQ, plays traditional music. At the age of 16, she was told she would make a good DJ. The early prediction came true. Today, among the many hats she wears, Jennie, the bluegrass traditionalist is a DJ at WPAQ. (see Appendix III Beyond MAin...Historic Radio Stations)

She broadcasted, "The radio is important to rural America." Kelly Epperson, the radio station owner, further added, "It is a viable way of communication in a small town." He taught Jennie, "Many of the people listening to the radio have no family, you are their family, you are their companion. It is like you are having a conversation with them. You connect with them"

For years, she has connected to her audience. People call in and make requests. She discovers their name, what they like, and what is happening in their life. Over time, she gets to know them, and they know her, like a familiar friend. Frequently, the listeners ask about her family. They care about her, and she cares about them.

The on-air personality has other station duties as well. She handles social media, represents the station at public events, selects the musical lineup, produces ads, answers the phone, and anchors the daily news. The astute businesswoman also owns a store.

Years ago, a local businessman, Bob Menicke, noticed the young waitress' talent, strength, and musical ability. He encouraged her to make a leap of faith to purchase a music store. With support from her family and a banking miracle, Jennie paid the down payment.

The first few months were shaky. For the next 12 months, she struggled. With tears filling her eyes, and pure honesty, Jennie shared, "I was not prepared for what would happen." The busy new owner had long toilsome days, and added to that, she started a new family.

A short time after buying the business, she lost her main support, her dad passed. And next, she lost the help of an experienced business owner who promised to be with her as she built a stable financial foundation for the new adventure. Only one person remained on staff.

"I could not have made it without Rick," she confirmed. "I connected to Rick" He was an employee of the store when she purchased it, and he became her husband. "I didn't realize it at the time but connecting to Rick allowed me to have all that I have now."

With the voice of experience, she firmly said, "Some people think owning a business is all flowers and rainbows, I'm telling you…business is hard… but we made it work."

She believes there are steps in life you must go through. A successful business just does not happen, there is more to it. She said, "I feel like God put people in my life, people I could connect with to further my life. Sometimes you do not realize how important connections are until you look back and see how it all worked out."

Eighteen years after the young woman opened the doors, The Olde Mill Music Store on Main Street continues. The store has everything you need to make music, from instruments and accessories to sound equipment. Her husband, a talented musician, provides expertise in sound systems. Master musicians teach in the studio.

The owner glowingly said, "I get enjoyment when people take a class, and I see them change, they are not the same person. I see them connect." She further confirmed, "We are here to make the connection."

Connection helps you overcome adversity. She proved that a strong woman connected to community rises to the top. With contentment, she spoke, "It is a pleasure to come to work every day! Each day, I see friendly people walking on Main Street."

Each day she is connected to family. She acknowledged. "I could not make it one day without mom, and my husband."

Her mom shares equal admiration. The retired music teacher and community choir director proudly said, "Jennie has a gift. Everyone has music in them, but some people have a gift." The musically seasoned mom, who has seen a lot of star performers, spoke about her daughter's uniqueness. "There is something about her, she has "it", she easily "connects" with the band." Few people surpass her as a rhythm guitarist." Her mom went on to say. "I'm proud of her. You couldn't ask for anyone any better." (see Appendix III Beyond MAin...Community Large Musical Groups)

Proudly connected to her past, Jennie honors the Lowry family who has been in Mount Airy since the 1800s. Like Jennie, they were business owners and contributed to the community. Her great-grandfather, JD Lowry, owned a printing store and organ manufacturing company, once located two blocks from her store. (see Appendix II More on

MAin...Lowry Park)

Thinking about her past, she feels you must connect to people before you lose the chance. Our family history is lost if we do not keep records and capture the oral tradition

Fully accessing her life, she acknowledged. "I don't want to move to a big city like Nashville, to make it big -- to be around my family is priceless." She continued. "For me, I cannot imagine doing anything differently, I respect and understand other people's choices but for me local connection is important."

It is clear, connecting to community is her happy place.

Jennie is concerned that many people are missing the opportunity. Many focus on the wrong thing while losing the chance to connect.

Wrapping up our conversation, she said, "I love my hometown. I love the connection I have with the people. I love serving them."

Our small town is an easy place to get connected.

Rick Caudill and Jennie Lowry
at Ole Mill Music Store

Dream...Roger Lineberry

On Main Street, I saw Michael Jackson!

The metallic military-styled jacket, the signature black fedora, the tight bundle of black curls dangling over his face, and the trademark single-sequined glove captured my attention.

I watched as he grabbed his crotch while doing a side slide, followed by a quick toe kick. Then cleanly executing the iconic spin, he broke into a robot dance, ending the performance with a moonwalk.

From across the street, I gaped. I had been transfixed, watching it all as if in another world. I had witnessed authentic passion.

Like thousands of visitors to Mount Airy, I had just witnessed a tribute artist execute a street show. Someone in the crowd nearby identified him as Roger Lineberry, the Michael Jackson of Mount Airy. (see Appendix II More on MAin, Tribute Artists)

For twelve years, the sidewalks of downtown have been Roger's stage as he impersonates the King of Pop. With his small boom box and his identifiable costume, he was easily recognized. Some laughed, others admired him, all the children loved him, and everyone was entertained. I was intrigued.

After witnessing his performance for the first time, a few months passed before I had the opportunity to have a conversation with him.

I attended a karaoke night sponsored by Rick Hunter, one of our local entrepreneurs. Rick is well-liked and respected in the community. He leads a Downtown Life Reinvented Group, teaching people how to dream of a better life and live life to the fullest. Rick was also instrumental in launching downtown's popular karaoke scene.

At the karaoke event, I saw Roger perform another Michael Jackson routine. That night, while talking with him, I discovered that he has a dream. I also realized that Roger is living life to the fullest.

Life had not been kind to him. Born into poverty, as a child, he knew conflict, neglect, and abuse. He was disowned and abandoned by his family. Alone, he walked around the neighborhood asking for food. Because he was different, other kids made fun of him and some bullied him.

Salvation was found in his grandmother. She took him in and nurtured him. He says those few years are filled with loving memories. His grandmother was a gospel singer and sang in different local churches. He started singing and traveled with her. It was the first time he felt like he had a purpose and the first time he felt love and acceptance. But the good time did not last.

Once again, life became dark. He was only 11 when his grandmother died. With no one to care for him, he was alone, again. Soon, he entered foster care. For a couple of years, he felt like an object floating aimlessly on a turbulent sea. During that interlude, he did not sing. His melody was smothered.

Roger Lineberry

At the age of 13, he discove Isolating himself in his room at the foster home, he constantly listened to the music and studied the lyrics of the King of Pop for two years. He began to identify with Jackson's lack of a childhood. Just like the performer, Roger felt misunderstood.

An uncanny connection with the superstar developed. "It was like I felt what Michael suffered," He said. He understood the deep meaning of the singer's powerful lyrics. The lyrics spoke to him.

He became familiar with many of the words and phrases and began to use them in conversation. The night of our detailed interview, he injected many of Michael's lyrics about peace, love, inclusion, and healing into our conversation. "I believe in the message of love and world peace," he said.

He was inspired by Jackson's dream to change the world with love and to make it a better place for all humanity. He became tirelessly committed to practicing and learning the star's iconic dance moves. He started to sing again. He committed to rehearsal.

At the age of 15, he took his dance skills and dream outside of his room and started performing. However, it was not until Michael's death in 2009 that Roger's dance exploded with passion. The death of the pop star intensified Roger's dream, adding the desire to keep the star's legacy alive.

His dedication to the dream possessed his life. He became laser focused and extremely passionate about his dance and Michael's legacy. His dream "to make the world a better place with music and dance" crystallized. Borrowing his idol's words, he explained, "To change the world you must first change the man in the mirror." He further affirmed, "I don't dance for money, but I dance to heal the world. My dance comes from God. If you cannot dance like me, you can do something to change the world."

Our chat was interrupted when they called him to the front to perform. Just like a seasoned artist, he strutted to the stage.

While he danced, I thought back to all the events and festivals where I had seen Roger perform. He worked the sidewalks during Art Walks, Cruise Ins, Girls' Night Out, 4th of July, and Christmas Parades; and at Truck Fest, Bud Break Wine & Craft Beer Festival, Mayberry Days®, and Autumn Leaves Festival. I saw him performing in the streets. I thought back to the first time I had seen him, dancing his heart out for a small crowd of onlookers. Almost any day, at any time, one could find Roger performing for any audience of any size.

When his performance at the karaoke show ended, our conversation continued. We talked more about his hopes for the world. He said that he dreamed of getting an agent, dancing professionally, and taking his message all over the world.

Nine months after our interview, he took a giant step toward his dream and moved to Morecambe, England. Morecambe is a coastal town on the Irish Sea. It is primarily a seaside resort community with a large portion of the local economy based on tourism, much like Mount Airy.

The city's population is five times larger than our little town. Today, he is dancing in the beach town's center, where, each day, hundreds of people witness his work to make the world a better place through music and dance.

Across the pond, Roger continues to dream. His world tour has begun.

Everyone has a dream. Dreams vary from mounds to mountains. Regardless of the dream, a first step is required.

Roger took his first steps from an underprivileged beginning, and overcame roadblocks, by focusing on his dream.

What is your dream? You can overcome adversity; you can fulfill your dream. Take your first step. Regardless of the size of your dream, take your first step.

Or, like Roger, take your first dance. Start with the person in the mirror. Let your dream make you – and the

world – better.
    Dreams come true in our small town.

65

Encouraging...Bill Hiatt

The professionally dressed man walked with an air of confidence. Bill noticed he was coming closer. As he approached, the unfamiliar man spoke.

"I was in your 8th-grade class. I know I didn't work hard, and I acted like I didn't care, but you kept talking to me, you kept encouraging me." The successful man recalled his teacher repeating, more times than he could remember, words of encouragement. With a smile as big as Texas, the confident man said, "I am a manager at a major hardware store, you encouraged me to push ahead and to do something with my life."

The man was no longer the underperforming middle-grade boy who was thinking about quitting school. He was a grown man who worked his way up in the business world and currently managing a store with sales of over 37 million dollars each year.

This reunion brought special satisfaction. Sitting at a small table at Snappy Lunch, while recalling the story, he was feeling fulfilled. Bill Hiatt continued to share with me from his heart, "I knew he could do something great, and I encouraged him to try hard in life, but I didn't know how far he would go. I am pleasantly surprised."

Bill had taught hundreds of young men and women, just like he did this former student, inspiring each of them to reach higher. He felt his life's purpose was to encourage them, telling them they could be successful in life.

Although a retired educator, he remains connected to his roots, he never traveled far from the farm, in the Sheltontown community, located only four miles from downtown Mount Airy. (see Appendix III Beyond MAin...Communities and Towns in Surry County)

Hard work and farming tobacco put food on the table.

"It was our way of life. I loved it." He spoke with pride. He further shared how respect, honor, and good neighboring were taught in the community. He remembers valuable encouragement from his family, the elders, and the church. "The older folks always had good advice and said something that could help you." He affirmed. He feels lucky to have been surrounded by so many encouragers.

Happy on the farm, Bill did not see his potential but one of his high school coaches did. The coach encouraged Bill to reach higher.

Surry County native, Bill's high school coach, minor league baseball player, and the most successful basketball coach in Catawba College history, Sam Moir was one of many who influenced him to be successful. Bill recognizes him as the one that inspired him to go to college.

With a teaching degree, Mr. Hiatt became an admired educator, teaching life skills to middle school students. He spurred hundreds of young people, sparking them to reach for the stars.

He retired from teaching twenty years ago, but he never stopped dispensing words of encouragement. At the age of 75, cemented as an encourager, he continues to touch as many lives as ever.

Currently serving as a personal care assistant at Central Continuing Care, he believes aging adults need encouragement. Some elderly people just need relief from daily pain, while others see their days getting shorter. Whatever the challenge, he tries to keep each person he works with thinking positively. "I'm older now, and I know how hard it is to keep positive." He said with compassion. (see Appendix III Beyond MAin...Retirement Communities and Nursing Facilities)

He remembers encouraging one 92-year-old woman living in a difficult situation, filled with pain, and distorted with anger. Her challenges caused her to become crusty. With a positive attitude, he designed a plan to make her days more enjoyable. Soon a connection was made, and trust developed. Her spirit softened. His accomplishment was noticed by friends and family. He was asked to speak at her funeral.

Bill loves to talk, and he speaks with scores of people every week at Floyd's Barber Shop. The shop originally opened in 1929 and moved in 1947 to its current location on Main Street. Formerly known as the City Barber Shop, it was renamed in 1980 and became officially Floyd's Barber Shop. Bill's dad owned the shop and knew Andy. Bill keeps the original equipment in the shop. (see Appendix II More on MAin – Replicas of the Andy Griffith Show).

Many families with young people come into the shop to take pictures and look around. Bill makes a special effort to encourage each of them to get a good education and to be the best they can be.

The riches found in his childhood community, and the positive influences through school enabled him to develop a gentle spirit with a desire to encourage and support everyone he meets on his journey through life.

Each person's journey includes challenging times. Bill shared a time of great testing.

His wife, JoAnn passed in 2012. Three years prior, she began to fight a battle with cancer. "It was a tough two and a half years. We have in our mind that our spouse will be with us always." He wistfully said.

With resilience, he continued. "I found encouragement from my close community that I have had since my youth. Grandparents, parents, family, friends, neighbors, and church family all inspired me to be positive. They encouraged me to look at life's blessings." He acknowledged, through the years, these powerful people gave him strength and impetus to change things for the better.

While we enjoyed our breakfast at Snappy Lunch, I was persuaded, he truly is an encourager. So, I asked, "Is there anything or anyone else that keeps you encouraged or positive?"

Without hesitation, he replied. "The people who come in the barbershop from all over the US and other countries inspire me. You can tell, they care about family, friends, and neighbors. The moral message on the Show inspires them. They have the attitude to keep the spirit of Mayberry going. It is amazing. It reminds me the world is filled with good people."

Speaking of good people, he wanted to boast about his children. Both, his son, and his daughter are good citizens in the community. They both treat people with respect and demonstrate brotherly love. His son gave him one of the greatest compliments he has ever gotten. He told him he wanted to raise his children just like he had been raised.

Thinking about his son's compliment, I began to contemplate what advice he might give. So, I asked, "What is the most important thing you say to encourage others?"

Wisdom began to flow, as he responded with a seasoned reply. "If you want to make the most out of life, look at everything in a positive way. Turn anything negative into a positive. Do good for other people. Doing good will help you as much to be happy as anything else. You will have ups and downs, but good will come if you work at it. Look at different angles, do not be pessimistic, purge negativity, and make each situation positive. Encourage others to be positive."

He concluded by saying, "I don't always remember words, but I always remember feelings. When people encourage you, you remember that feeling, and you will remember them forever."

Bill's story is one of the reasons people flock to Mount Airy. And when they come, they are encouraged by his gentle words, uplifted by his kind smile, and inspired by his twinkling eyes.

Encouragement can be found in our small town.

I Samuel 30:6 David was greatly distressed......but he encouraged himself in the Lord.

Bill Hiatt in Floyd's Barbershop

Family...Jenny Smith

It may have been the grandest Valentine's Party of all time. Due to the girls' entertaining appearance, the event was nicknamed the "Ophelia and Everly Tea Party".

From a distance, Ophelia's cotton white hair looked like fluffy whipped cream. A glimmering "grandma-style" sweater accented her lavender dress. The long strap of her pocketbook hung over her shoulder. The circular wire-rimmed glasses perched on her nose matched her rounded rosy cheeks.

Everly's curly grey hair circled her head in the shape of a perfectly rounded melon. Her glasses sat on her face attached by a golden chain. The knitted sweater perfectly matched the carnation pink two-piece outfit with white hosiery.

They both gave the classic look of a senior citizen, but the one-year-olds were little girls in wigs.

They were a hit in the healthcare facility, where Ophelia's great-grandmother resided. Their popularity began before the party, dressed in their costumes, they had been viewed by over two million people on Facebook.

You might think it was planned for them to be the main attraction at the party, but Jenny, Ophelia's mother organized the party for another lady, her grandma Tickle, and grandma outshined the little girls by acting like the "belle of the ball" and rightly so because she was the queen of the event.

As the norm, Jenny's family rallied around the matriarch as her health declined. Before her being placed in the facility, every day, one or more of the family members visited her home, took care of her needs, and prepared her meals. She became so weak, and her health failed to the point that assisted nursing care was required. Daily, the family continued to visit, supporting her, while she received medical care.

During this difficult time, Virginia Kathleen Smith (Jenny), the granddaughter, who is the crafty one of the family, led them in creating a memory that warmed the heart for a lifetime.

The women of the family are known for being strong leaders; Jenny is one of them. She was named after two powerful women, one from each side of the family, Grandma Kathleen, and Grandma Virginia.

The young strong woman is a mover and shaker and well-connected in the community. She is experienced in hospitality and tourism. Professionally, she is the Visitor Center and Group Tour Manager for Mount Airy Visitors Center. (see Appendix II More on MAin...Mount Airy Visitors Center)

As an influencer, she serves on several local boards and committees: Mount Airy Downtown Business Association; Mount Airy Recreation Commission, Mount Airy Appearance Commission, Mount Airy Relocation and Retirement Committee, Surry County's 250th Anniversary Committee, and the Mount Airy Museum of Regional History. Although busy, she makes time for family, especially time for grandma.

The grandmother had only been in the facility for a few days, when Jenny, along with two of her cousins, her aunts, and her mom, planned a Tea Party with Valentine crafts (it was two weeks till Valentine's Day). All the residents in the healthcare facility were invited. Jenny's community business friends helped. Rosie with the Groovy Goose, a vintage boutique gave old-fashioned hats to wear, and Angela with Miss Angels Heavenly Pies gave the desserts. (see Appendix II More on MAin...Groovy Goose and More on MAin...Miss Angel's Heavenly Pies)

No shortcuts were taken, as the party planners rallied together to adorn the party room with dazzling decorations using handmade pastel hearts. They designed an easy-to-make craft allowing everyone to create a door wreath made from various hues of pink and red cut-out-paper hearts. The staff decorated the tables and added other special touches. Everyone attending the party was given a special teacup.

The celebratory atmosphere was like a fresh breath of air which helped reduce the stress of caregiving and lifted the spirits of those who were sick. Joyful laughter rang out as smiles formed on glowing faces. Softly playing in the background, a classic list of love songs enhanced the event. For an afternoon, life took over sickness, laughter replaced sadness and family reclaimed peace.

For as long as the grieving party planner could remember, her loved ones gathered, supporting each other during the events of life and death. They were present pillars, propping each other up through sicknesses, births, graduations, birthdays, parties, celebrations, disappointments, and deaths.

Grandpa Tickle had served as a role model, revealing how a true family man leads. He demonstrated to his children and grandchildren how to love and how to take care of a wife and family. She said, "Grandma depended on him, and she was lost at his passing."

In widowhood, as her health grew frailer, the tight-knit family stepped in. The closeness of the family was experienced throughout the challenging five years of caregiving. Their bond made the Valentine's Party planning easy.

After the party, in less than two weeks, they rallied again, this time for her funeral.

As the mourners gathered in grandma's home, they reminisced. One of the children made a statement about all the garments that she had in the "big room". Over time, the purpose of the room became a storage place. The vast assortment of clothing and accessories filled the converted room serving as a walk-in closet. The children did not know if she wore most of the clothes packed in the room, it was more like a collection. Over the years, the little kids of the family had fun playing dress up in her 'closet'. There were so many interesting and fun things to see and wear.

In an elegant, snazzy, and fun way, she could have been considered a flashy lady. Her style was full of pizazz. She endlessly shopped for bargains and searched thrift stores collecting beautiful things and bright jazzy jewelry.

The day before the funeral, as the adult grandkids entered the room, they gazed at the vast amount of trendy clothing, remembering all the good times, it warmed their hearts. Someone noted how there were a lot of fur coats.

The chatter began, and the ideas ran like race cars around a track. It appeared there were enough fur coats for each of them to wear one. One grandchild suggested the idea, and they all agreed, this would be a fitting memory – fur-filled funeral", fondly remembering Grandma.

On Valentine's Day, the family came together (including Jenny's dad's side of the family) one more time to honor and celebrate the life of a loved one who had passed.

Five daughters, a daughter-in-law, and seven grandchildren, elegantly walked into the funeral home, each one proudly wearing one of her fur coats. Each descendant was adorned with decorative pieces of ornamental jewelry, all from the matriarch's collection. The furs and glitzy costume jewelry were in honor and memory of their voguish grandma.

In the next ten days, two more times, the family proved to be invaluable. Her uncle by marriage passed, and her cousin would be married. Through it all, the family was there, to mourn or to celebrate. "We've always been close; we've always been there for each other, and we always will be," Jenny said.

"I was in college, away from home and away from family, when I realized how good it is to have family," she recalled. "Family is the most important thing in life," with firm confidence, she gently declared, "they will be there no matter what." They might not agree with a decision you make and what you are doing but they will be there."

Being an only child, Jenny grew up closely surrounded by a large family, including 20 cousins. She grew even closer to her family when she married. Jonathan her husband, helped redefine what family means to her, giving life and family greater meaning.

Being a strong family man, he fits perfectly into the clan. His parents died while they were dating. During those difficult times of sickness and loss, she witnessed the love and care that he gave.

After his dad passed, he helped his mom through her sickness. The couple spent their New Year's Eve date in the hospital, celebrating with mom. "He was so caring and helpful," The bride-to-be said, "I knew he was a family man." As the soon-to-be-married couple grew closer, he drew closer to her family.

After their marriage, four years later, his brother passed. Through it all, he was there for his dad, mom, and brother. How he served his loved ones during that time made her cherish family even more.

As her eyes filled with tears of love and emotion, in a broken voice she spoke, "Family became even more precious to me when my daughter, was born. Becoming a mom is the best thing that ever happened to me. And being blessed twice, with two beautiful daughters, has made my heart complete. It literally feels like my heart could burst at any moment when I'm looking at my girls. It's a love like no other and one that I want to cherish and never take for granted. Family is important to me," she stated with persuasion.

Jenny loves spending time with Jonathan, Ophelia, and Charlotte, she tells them every day that she loves them. She concluded our conversation with the following statement: "I value family so much, and I love them so much it hurts."

Jenny, Her Husband, Daughters, and Parents

Mother Teresa said, "I have found the paradox, that if you love until it hurts, there can be no more hurt, only more love." Enduring, real love requires sacrifice, sacrifice can be painful as you give from your own "need" (not surplus) whether it is resources of strength or wealth. But as Mother Teresa discovered, the more you give (even in sacrifice) the more you receive.

Life lessons learned from true family are "Give more love and you will receive more love" and "Be the best family member you can be, and you will have the best family there is".

Close-knitted families filled with love adorn our small town and often gather at grandma's house on Sundays.

Friends...Esther Johnson

My life was changed forever by her spiritual beauty.

Over forty-five years ago, I was honored with the privilege of gaining a sage in my life who became one of my most trustworthy friends. Her name is Frances Draughn, a lady filled with great light and grace.

The firstborn of Frances is Esther Draughn Johnson. The name Esther stems from the Persian word *setareh,* which means star. She too is a great light from whom I draw inspiration. She, like her mother, became and continues to be a treasured friend.

Through decades of life's transitions, we were geographically separated by hundreds of miles, but our friendship never oscillated. After many years of not seeing her, I sauntered into the Mount Airy Visitors Center on a luminous Wednesday morning. She greeted me with lively laughter, loyal love, and an old-fashioned maternal hug.

Her eyes twinkled with a glorious smile. She gleamed with joy. Immediately, our conversation ignited with excitement. During our talkfest, I discovered she knew almost everything about Mount Airy and it appeared she knew everyone.

She is an authentic true friend. Over time, I discovered she is real, reliable, and respectful. She has style and portrays herself as a confident woman. She embraces life by squeezing out the essence and joy of each minute. Her unforgettable laugh gushes from a canyon of joyfulness. Her presence is uplifting.

Her colorful personality is compatible with the kaleidoscopic of characters in "Mayberry", aka Mount Airy. She is passionate in her pursuit to connect with people which enables her to be a proficient greeter at the Visitors Center.

The thousands of people who visit our active small town each year remember her as the pleasant lady with a huge smile. Brimming with charm, she is the perfect person to welcome you to our amiable little town.

She is active in the community. She is the President of the Surry County Genealogical Society; she teaches Beginning Genealogy classes, and she is our regional ancestry expert.

She is a benevolent woman of faith and well-connected to many of our area non-profits. She is the lady of grace about town. She is one of our small town's delightful socialites.

If you need to network or if you need any kind of information, she is a wellspring of information that flows with knowledge.

After retiring back to Mount Airy, I made visiting with Esther a frequent event. The times I spend with her are like sitting at the feet of *Gamaliel* (a great first-century teacher). I gain wisdom from the golden words that flow from her lips.

Her witticisms are plentiful and diverse: "Do better every day; Set examples for others; If you make a mistake, try to do better; Nobody is perfect in this world; If it is fun, do it, just have fun; and Everybody has a story to tell." Her philosophy of life is the golden rule, "Do unto others as you would have them do to you."

She articulates proverbial wisdom like a farmer scattering seeds. During one of our warm conversations, with a calm upbeat confidence, she slowly and cheerfully said, "Everybody is your friend you just don't know it." After watering this statement with meditation, I allowed it to grow and become rooted in how I see people.

No matter who you are, she is the type of person that makes you feel better after being in her presence. With ease, she connects with the young and old. In her own words, she is easy to get along with, not bad to fuss, and does not talk badly about anyone.

One time I told her how much I cherished our friendship and I expressed how she is always cheerful. To which she giggled and said, "If you fuss people will stay away from you."

Adored by her family and loved by her husband, she is affectionately called the boss (mostly by her husband). With a twinkle in her eye and a high-pitched one-of-a-kind voice, she chuckled, "I am the oldest child, and the oldest child has to be the boss."

Developing a friendship with her is uncomplicated. Without effort, she brings you into a warm and caring relationship. There is no wonder she has over 3000 friends on Facebook and more friends of flesh than you can count.

Esther Johnson
Between the Fun Girls of Mount Pilot, Dixie, Andy Griffith's daughter and Michelle Bryson

Having friends is one of the greatest things you can do to enhance your life. The Irish say that a friend is like a four-leaf clover; hard to find but lucky to have. People with friends are lucky.

The philosopher Aristotle said, "In poverty and other misfortunes of life, true friends are a sure refuge."

Friends provide great support and help fill the basic needs of life. The Mayo Clinic staff printed in a Healthy Lifestyle's online article that friends improve health and overall well-being. Without friends, we become isolated. Loneliness and isolation contribute to poor health. Other studies have shown that friendships play a key role in health and happiness – especially as we get older. With so many friends, no wonder, Esther is such a happy person.

Friends are especially valuable in difficult times. Proverbial wisdom teaches us that friends stick closer than a brother. Jesus, the master teacher transformed a system of 'leader and follower' into a community of friends. He identified them with a new label, he said, "You are my friends."

There is a lot of scientific literature and evidence that supports the value of friendships. The case has been made. The data is clear. Having friends in your life is good for you.

A friend like Esther has been incredibly good for me, and a true friend will be good for you.

My wise grandmother, Maude Vaughn, told me that if I had two or three real friends, I would be a rich man. I heard someone else say it is better to eat French fries with a friend than to eat broccoli alone.

Did I mention eating? Recently, Esther and I went out for a friendly meal on "restaurant row". Restaurant row is a one-mile stretch of Rockford Street, where 31 restaurants, three hotels, and shopping are located. (see Appendix III Beyond MAin...Restaurant Row)

She and I were in no hurry. We enjoyed the time together. She had eaten earlier in the day and was not very hungry, so she only ordered ice cream. She loves ice cream. When asked by the waiter how many scoops, she smiled, and said, "Two scoops definitely!"

I think two-scoops suggest a lot about a person. It shows a person knows how to enjoy life by living on a mountain of refreshing satisfaction. I think when someone doubles up on pleasure, it demonstrates you know how to live life to the fullest by doubling joy. (see Appendix III Beyond MAin...Ice Cream Shops)

My friend, Esther, lives her life with all the joy that can be scooped onto the platter of life. Friends like Esther are some of life's greatest riches and more refreshing than ice cream.

Solomon, the proverbial author said, "A friend loves at all times." Anyone would be blessed to have a true friend and any of us would be more blessed if we learned to be a true friend.

Remember the wit of Esther, 'everyone is your friend'. It is important to recognize the value of each person. Each person we meet is a potential friend. Friends are priceless.

There is no better place than Mount Airy, with its small-town charm, to make or be a friend.

Hope...Emma Jean Tucker

She whispered. "I'm still riding hope." The next day, Rosa Green Tucker passed. The matriarch had planted seeds of hope that helped her six children become optimistic, accomplished, and valued citizens of the world. Like her five siblings, Emma Jean allowed the heritage of hope from her mother to brightly guide her future.

Although a descendant of slavery, her mother's forward-thinking was not chained. She was courageous and smart. Honoring the value of every human, she embraced equality. She tightly held the ideal that *if someone else can do it I can too*.

Emma Jean remembers an event during the days of segregation when her spunky mother was shopping downtown. A discriminatory policy prevented her from trying on a hat.

As her mom picked up a hat, viewing the potential purchase, a store clerk reminded her of the ridiculous rule. With a spirited response, she placed the hat on her head and confidently replied, "My hair is just as clean as the others trying on the hats."

On the way home, the newly purchased dainty headpiece had a special place to rest on the car seat and in the heart.

The Tucker home was filled with hope for a better day, and education would be a key to open doors of opportunity. Education was valued, school attendance was required, and home study was given emphasis. "If you can learn the songs on the radio, you can learn your spelling words." Her mom would say. No excuse to fail was allowed and for the lazy learner a gentle pop with a ruler followed by "I don't know much but you are going to know as much as I do."

Emma Jean is a former student of the state-of-the-art

historic Rosenwald School and a graduate of the local historic JJ Jones School. Both were notable schools for African American children during the early 20th century. The legendary teachers at the high school are celebrated by many former students for inspiring hope. (see Appendix III Beyond Main Street...African American History)

Hope sparks innovation. Despite the limited opportunities in a small town and the added challenges of being a minority, the hopeful Tucker family prospered through hard work and educational pursuits.

James, the patriarch of the farming family commuted to West Virginia to work in the mines.

When the children were small, the self-determined mom wanted to upgrade the kitchen and add heat to the house. But money was tight. After learning of a prospect in New York, the spunky mom worked out a plan to temporarily work in Long Island and came back with enough money to upgrade the home and buy nice towels and pretty things for the kitchen.

Forty-five years after the renovations, the fourth child, Emma Jean Tucker, a retired educator lives in the ole' home place.

She invited me to share a meal. I pulled into the driveway and immediately, I saw hope.

Rustic wood signs with the word "hope" were thoughtfully placed on the sides of the shed that looked like a tiny house. Looking to the left, yard signs were planted, sending the same message. Upon entering the home, hope adorned the warm country décor. After a delightful lunch, she began to share her story.

"A small child doesn't always understand the full picture, but in my youth, hope grew into dreams." She revealed. "Although the word teacher was not in my childlike vocabulary, I dreamed." Her early interest hinted at her lifelong profession as an educator. "I always collected and amused myself with papers. Writing was a favorite activity. I played school with my dolls."

Although school was a hopeful place, the fair-complected third grader found it was also a place of hurt. "I began to experience mean girls, and what my grandmother called ugly behavior. They called me names because of my complexion and talked about my hair. They said I have hair like straw. It affected my life so much that when I grew up, I would dye my hair black. As I matured, I began to understand that hurting people hurt people."

Added to the pain of ridicule, her school had no library, and no new books and the building was barely more than a frame. Tangible things were lacking but the school was filled with inspiring teachers. One teacher noticed her academic interests and achievements and encouraged her to go to college. Emma Jean had no plans to go to college. But the praise lifted her spirit and sparked a desire to become a teacher.

The climate of segregation tried to muffle hope. She recalls, "I couldn't even go into the drug store to sit down." Another time she remembers, driving an old '49 Fluid Drive with her small siblings in the car, she remembers stopping at a roadside cafe for curbside service on HWY 89, "We don't serve colored." They barked. Without service, she drove away.

She fondly recalls, every second Sunday, the family going to church, and stopping at the Dairy Center. Daddy would have to go to the window for pickup and bring the soft serve ice cream to the car. She remembers thinking, one day I hope to go in there. (see Appendix III Beyond Main...Diary Center)

Outside of Mount Airy, other barriers to hope attempted to muffle promising dreams. In her Junior year, she rode the Greyhound bus to New Jersey with a stop in South Boston, Virginia. Imprinted in her mind is the White Only sign for the bathroom and water fountain. In those days, persons of color overcame by traveling with food and a jug of water because they did not know if they could stop and get any.

Reflecting, she recalls her sister warming the baby's bottles on the radiator because they were concerned there would be no safe place to stop while traveling.

The older folks in her community strengthened hope by saying one day things will get better. "I became confident, that one-day things would change for the better." She spoke with assurance.

She comes from a long line of hopeful people. Her great-grandparents hoped to be free and own land. Eventually, they became independent large farm owners by buying little parcels, one at a time. They always thought things would get better and they made it happen for them and their descendants.

Emma Jean said, "You have to have hope. You have got to look for the light at the end of the tunnel." One of her favorite authors, Emily Dickerson said, "Hope is the thing with feathers, that perches in the soul and sings the tune without words."

She embraces another saying quoted by Martin Luther King, Jr. He said, "If you don't have hope, you only have despair."

While a young adult, her life began to blossom. With only $25 and hope she was accepted at Cheyney State College, Cheyney, PA. As a working student during the summers, along with family sacrifices opportunity grew into purpose.

Unique connections watered her journey with success. Hopeful people always lift you higher. Soon after getting a degree in education, she moved to San Francisco, then returned to plant herself on the east coast.

Her first teaching job was in Wilmington Delaware. It was a wonderful experience. Next, she moved to Newark, Delaware. She loved the classroom and teaching elementary students. For the next 22 years, she thrived while fulfilling her dream. Her success as an educator was noticed.

She was recruited to develop a program for kindergarteners at risk for poor performance. She called it "Parent Partners". The program connected paraprofessionals with children in the classroom and helped the parents in the home support their child's learning. The successful program required exceeding long days filled with fatigue.

Emma Jean Tucker and Calvin
at the Rockford Historic Inn

During that time, her peers encouraged her to further her education. She pondered. "I didn't feel like I had the time and strength to complete another degree." Ignoring her gentle protests, her supervisor placed her in a less stressful position, making it easier to go to graduate school. The struggle required small steps but eventually, success was achieved.

After earning a master's degree, her career expanded. She implemented an innovative national program called "Parents as Teachers". Ms. Tucker led the program statewide.

Looking back, she sees the roots of hopeful inspiration not only through her mother but also her dad. "My wonderful daddy was wise, fair, kind, gentle, and encouraging. He was a great provider." He was resourceful and worked in coal mines and managed a farm that sold to the community and to businesses. He taught the children how to earn a dollar through hard work.

While contemplating retirement, she could not think of a better place to retire than Mount Airy. Her roots run deep on the 100-acre farm. She became the steward of the family property.

Not long after retiring, she became inspired to redo her grandparents' house which was built in 1914. The house was built on land they purchased in 1871. The restoration became a family project, and all the siblings worked together to bring it back to life as a historical landmark. (see Appendix III Beyond Main...African American History)

She admitted that life changed in 2021, but she is firm in her belief that hope lives on.

"Covid-19 and current conflicts tried to dim our future". She spoke. Over half a million Americans have died, and the number grows by the thousands each day. Too many have resigned to the 'new normal', giving up, and thinking things will never be the same. We are dazed in the face of isolation, fear, and lifestyle changes that no one imagined, yet hope lives.

National statistics are discouraging, and despite growing poverty, unrest, crime, drug abuse, child abuse, battered lives, and increased suicides, hope lives. The anxiety and uneasiness in dark times have caused many to feel hopeless. Yet, with surety Emma Jean declared, "I am hopeful, things will get better. There is always hope"

The enduring success of our small town stands on these inspiring words, "I'm still riding hope."

Psalm 71:14 I will always have hope.

Tucker Home
Built-in 1914, Restored to Museum Quality

Imagination...Brack Llewelyn

A twig snapped, dark silence choked the night, and a piercing fear rushed through his soul. Wide and bright as the moon, the little boy's eyes fixated, peering into the woods. Like a soldier at attention, he sat straight up.

From the front porch, he slowly leaned toward the woods. With a peering pause, he thought he could see the ghost. His skin crawled and chills like ice water rippled down his spine. The fading phantom seemed as real as the haunting voice of the storyteller.

At least, this is how the guest speaker's story triggered my imagination. I could see young Brack Llewelyn as he experienced any one of the many ghost stories, his grandpa deposited into his tiny receptive ears. Each story was another jewel, that richly filled his creative mind with the treasures of imagination.

Recently, at the Granite City History Group meeting, Brack attributed the gift of his powerful imagination to his grandparents' storytelling. He said, "They were great storytellers."

Recalling his childhood, he continued to share that one of the most popular family activities (and his favorite) was to sit on the front porch in the evenings and listen to the sometimes inflated, many times funny, always intriguing, usually true, and often scary tales. He especially remembers the ghost stories. He said, "My grandfather was the best ghost teller, he made it all seem so real."

The ghost tales, which seemed so real to him, reminded me of the local folklore of our chilling past. Local haunting tales are dramatically presented downtown by our local Ghost Tour guides. (see Appendix II More on MAin...Tours)

His storytelling heritage filled with a colorful imagination and eerie tales was evident. Grandpa Llewelyn's natural ability for tall tales was always entertaining while his great-grandmother Sarah Bidnesa

Morgan Llewelyn's captivating stories were captured with the pen. "I accredit all of my creative imagination to them." He affirmed.

With vivid detail, he further described the rich oral history and written word that formed his artistry. He said, "There is power in storytelling, it sparks imagination."

He grew up in Dobson, North Carolina (today's population is 1,586), and the population was even smaller when he was a child. Dobson was established as the county seat of Surry County in 1853, replacing Rockford which is located on the edge of the Yadkin River. Historic Rockford is even smaller than Dobson. (see Appendix III Beyond MAin...Rockford and Beyond MAin...Communities and Towns in Surry County)

He was a student at the rural schools, and a graduate of Surry Central, one of the county's three high schools. He attended the University of North Carolina at Greensboro and graduated with an Arts Degree.

Since his youth, his talent has grown and creatively developed. Today, he is amazingly imaginative, artistically gifted, writes wonderfully, and communicates grandly.

Professionally, he has worked for the Surry Arts Council, Ridgecrest Retirement Community (one of the area's premier retirement communities), and the Mount Airy Senior Center (certified as A Center of Excellence by the North Carolina Division on Aging and Adult Services).

Being semi-retired, he continues to work part-time with WPAQ and WSYD (local radio stations). As a radio Disc Jockey, he is a music guru and prepares interesting background information on the songs and artists, as well as organizes entertaining musical-themed shows. He conducts interviews, records ads, and announces the news. (see Appendix III Beyond MAin...Historic Radio Stations)

In the performing arts arena, he writes, directs, and acts in numerous plays each year.

Currently, he and his talented wife of 25 years, Angela,

live in the Flat Rock area (the name stems from the community's granite quarry located nearby), just a couple of miles outside of Mount Airy. The granite quarry is the largest open-faced granite quarry in the world and has been mined since 1889. (see Appendix III Beyond MAin...Granite Quarry and Beyond MAin...Communities and Towns in Surry County)

Another man with imagination saw the granite in the quarry as more than a 'flat rock', although the farmers thought the land was useless, with imagination, the stoneman saw an industry that could last for 500 years.

The Donna Fargo Highway goes through the Flat Rock community, all the way to the childhood home of the local celebrity. She also had imagination. Her imagination carried her from a country farm to California, where she became a successful country singer-songwriter. (see Appendix III Beyond MAin...Donna Fargo)

Many successful and famous people call Mount Airy home, and all of them demonstrate the power of imagination. Brack Llewellyn is one of them. (see Appendix IV Famous People From Mount Airy)

He is extremely creative. Much of the growth in our community's lively performing arts scene has been enriched by his work.

He and his wife, with imagination, created a theatrical entertainment company, The Nonesuch Players. The company performs plays, utilizing the talent of locals. He is the idea person who ignites the artistic vision and purposely remains in the background so other people's talents and gifts can shine.

They perform dinner theatre, storytelling, stage shows, and specific themed events. They do public and private events, and school performances, and will even perform in your living room. To the company, the world is a stage. Brack said, "We do it all."

Angela, along with his support, developed a local acting

group for teens at the library, called the Dewey Decimal Players. Sometimes they do collaborative performances. The teen group often feeds their actors directly into the Nonesuch Players. (see Appendix III Beyond MAin...Live Theatre and Performers)

Recently, they performed on Main Street, just before the annual 4th of July parade. In period costumes and characters, they assumed the role of citizens of the American Revolution. While hearing the Declaration of Independence being read, they acted as if they were hearing it for the first time. The streets swelled with observers who were drawn into the scene and felt as if they too were colonial citizens. The street show concluded with thunderous applause.

Since 2001, the Nonesuch Players have performed over 100 plays and over 216 benefit performances (raising thousands of dollars for area nonprofits). Most of the performed plays were written by Brack. He acted in many of them. All were staged and directed by him and Angela.

Added to the full performance schedule, he found time to do storytelling for cancer survivors, assist the Downtown Redevelopment Group plan events and he formed a successful Reader's Theatre Group at Ridgecrest Retirement Community. He is often the first face you see at citywide events (serving as Master of Ceremonies). He always brings excitement and seasoned entertainment to our parades and celebrations.

One of the greatest things about him is that people connect with him, building lifelong friendships. The community admires and respects his craft. "I just do what I love." He spoke with passion. He inspires imagination in others who want to become better artists.

Storytelling ignites the imagination. Imagination is powerful, it creates greatness. It sees a rock and establishes a quarry. It conceives a melody and writes a hit song.

An old man with imagination develops a story. He

skillfully delivers it on a front porch, keeping a little boy (with mouth wide open) on the edge of his seat. Then, with an arousing finale, a young creative mind ignites with creativity that captivates, delights, and inspires thousands of people in the next generation.

Another boy had imagination that changed the destiny of a nation. Little David, from an exceedingly small town in Israel, and the least of his family, had life-changing imagination. The probable stories told by his dad, and perhaps the tales told by the other shepherds, fed his mind with creative thought. He looked at a giant but imagined opportunity.

Be a storyteller, you can ignite a mind to create amazing things.

Thanks to imaginative people like Brack who share their gifts and talents, our small town has an active performing arts scene.

Nonesuch Playmakers, Fourth of July Street Drama

Influence...Summer Shelton

Mount Airy native Summer Shelton is an accomplished producer. Her films have premiered at some of the world's most prestigious film festivals, including Sundance, Venice, Karlovy Vary in the Czech Republic, and Tribeca and New Directors/New Films in New York.

I think a book could be written recounting her childhood and journey. In this brief narrative, I highlight some of her accomplishments and identify what I see as the power of "influence".

She began a professional career as an associate producer on Ramin Bahrani's (director/screenwriter) award-winning 2008 drama, *Goodbye Solo.*

Since entering the film industry, she added credits to her work history as an associate producer on features (full-length films) and a co-producer on several film industry projects. Her subsequent credits include shorts (40-minute or less films) and an HBO mini-series documentary.

Her accomplishments as a producer and an executive producer have been recognized by her peers. She is the recipient of many impressive film awards.

Her recent major movie projects include producing *Keep the Change* and *Maine,* both of which premiered at the Tribeca Film Festival.

I think, the movie, *Keep the Change,* is influencing a generation. The romantic comedy has influenced how persons with disabilities (especially those on the autism spectrum) are represented in the movies. (see Appendix III Beyond MAin...Mount Airy Autism Society)

The director of the feature film, Rachael Israel, was influenced to make the movie based on the first serious romance of a longtime friend, who is on the autism spectrum. For authenticity, Israel required the lead actors to be on the "spectrum". This was a first in the movie industry.

The heartwarming plot is based on a true story of love that includes the unique interactions of family, friends, and a young couple's desire and pursuit of love. The audience is taken far into the storyline before they realize the dating couple, David, and Sarah, along with some of their friends are all on the "spectrum". To the end of the movie, some viewers may continue to question if the actors are on the "spectrum".

The movie shows the influence that love has on all people, regardless of who you are, where you come from, or what diagnosis you may have, we all desire to love and be loved.

The feature-length film began as a short for Israel's graduate school thesis project at Columbia University's School of the Arts. Her thesis mentor was director Ramin Bahrani whom Shelton had collaborated with on multiple projects. Bahrani connected the two filmmakers as he knew the project would speak to Shelton's artistic sensibilities. He would also serve as a Creative Consultant on the feature film.

I had a once-in-a-lifetime experience, when I saw a screening of the film at the Historic Earl Theatre, with producer, Summer Shelton. She introduced the movie, followed by a question-and-answer session. The event was thrilling and eye-opening. She is an amazing hometown girl who made it in the Big Apple.

The producer of the movie said, "I am what I am because of the small-town influence." She shared how she grew up on a family farm with wonderful parents. They lived in the Westfield community, located just a few miles from the city limits of Mount Airy.

Her parents, Chester, and Sandra Shelton were community influencers. Well-known in the community, they took a lead role in getting people involved in projects:

organizing an active Ruritan Club; restoration of an old schoolhouse to a functioning community building; and establishing a veteran memorial service and monument. Added to these accomplishments they guided the placement of a Westfield welcome sign, the building of a ballfield, a walkway, and many successful fundraisers for neighbors in need.

No doubt Summer was influenced by her adventurous and independent dad and her artistic mother who loved renting movies as an every weekend mother and daughter activity. Recalling those special times, her mom said, "I think, by the time Summer was old enough to watch a movie, we started the weekly tradition."

One of Summer's fondest memories, and I think a propelling influence contributing to her path to being a producer, is renting those movies at the Westfield Superette, now known as Jake's on Westfield Road. Nine miles out of Mount Airy, this small gas station, part grocery store, and key country hang-out was the only place to shop between the farm and town. (see Appendix III Beyond MAin...Communities and Towns in Surry County)

She described her early life as simple, further explaining how you do chores, go to school, and every Saturday you would clean the house. The farm girl attributed the hard work ethic she learned on the farm to her ability to make it in New York City.

To me, her childhood sounded routine. She went on to talk about how in a small town you have all kinds of different people. She said, "I went to school with the haves, the have-nots, and migrant workers, but it didn't matter we were all the same. We were all friends." She noted that having different zip codes did not matter on the farm. With sincerity, she said, "We are still just people." She warmly remembers, getting pop (soda/soft drink) and a pack of nabs (peanut butter snack crackers) and renting a movie on Saturday night. This was a major weekly event that hinted at the direction of her career.

From the farm, she went on to have a major life experience by going to film school at the North Carolina School of the Arts (UNCSA). During school, she worked as an intern, acted in bit parts, and made valuable connections.

As positive influences in her life grew, her desire to make movies gained courage. She said, "I got lucky." While studying at UNCSA, she began to work with critically acclaimed director Ramin Bahrani who was preparing his third feature film *Goodbye Solo* to shoot in Winston-Salem.

She reflects, "He became my mentor and teacher who greatly impacted my career. I worked alongside, Bahrani on *Goodbye Solo* (2008) as an Associate Producer and relocated to New York City after we completed the film." Their collaboration continued as they partnered on his fourth feature *At Any Price,* as well as short films *Plastic Bags* and *Eg Anda.*

This is only part of the journey that led Summer to become a full-time producer.

The night of the screening in Mount Airy, she humbly acknowledged her accomplishments. With honesty, she revealed there were challenges along the way.

In her career, she went on to work with more amazing filmmakers. She won more awards and notable fellowships. She met and networked with well-known artists.

She was honored in 2018 as the recipient of the prestigious Independent Spirit Piaget Producer's Award. The Award is given by Film Independent. The honor was established to recognize an emerging producer who, despite highly limited resources, demonstrates the creativity, tenacity, and vision required to produce quality independent films.

The New York Times reviewed the movie *Keep the Change* as a success, stating "It is a landmark movie..." In discussing the movie, Shelton said, "No matter where you come from, life is about love and making connections." She said, "I really like that the movie is about real people played by real people because, at the end of the day, we are all human."

Again, I think you can see the small-town experiences that aided in developing her viewpoint that love is the same for everybody.

The world's oldest Hebrew wisdom document written by a King said, "You use iron to sharpen iron, and one friend sharpens another." In other words, you influence others with your character, your abilities and by the environment you create.

In my opinion, you can easily see Summer's influences that affected the direction of her life. It all began with the sway of a small town, growing up on a farm, and learning country values.

The weekly movie rentals played a part in developing her growing hunger for the craft of filmmaking. I think there were other impactful events as well, such as art school connections, university support, and chance meetings which increased her courage to grow confidence to produce movies.

Each influencer in her life, just like dominos, allowed everything to fall into place for the making of *Keep the Change*. I feel, her progression to success stood on them.

Using the "spectrum" the movie supports the belief that love is the same for all people. As I noted earlier, the movie has the potential to influence a generation by changing the way people think about love.

Influence is powerful. It creates a changing course much like how a winding river's direction is affected by soft soil, as it plows through, redirecting its path. Each of us has the power to effect positive change, creating a more loving and accepting world by leading with influence.

All types of people who make up our small town are loved and valued and each one has the power of influence.

The story is based on the notes taken by the writer at the

Summer Shelton lecture at <u>Keep the Change</u> viewing as well as conversations with the producer. Additional information was taken from the following published articles: "Yes! Weekly 2018; New Orleans Film Society; UNCSA 2017; The Guardian 2018, SAG INDIE 2018 and the New York Times. The movie <u>Keep the Change</u> is available on Amazon.

Kindness...Jonathan Lightfoot

Only seven years old, he was asked one of the most important questions of his life. It determined his future. "Where would you like to live?" His mother asked.

Most little boys have a limited list of places to live, but not Jonathan. He had firsthand knowledge of many cities, multiple states, and several countries.

His mom was the first black Navy air traffic controller in the country. During her 20-year Navy career, she traveled the world. Her son became familiar with the many places she was stationed, and he lived with her in various locations around the country and learned about her overseas assignments.

His awareness of Japan, the Gulf states, Turkey, and the Virgin Islands gave him a world perspective. His exposure to Puerto Rico, California, Maryland, DC, and New Jersey added to his national awareness.

Although his attentive ears heard much about the various places his mother was assigned, the navy kid was not always allowed to travel with her. Sometimes when mom was deployed, a loving, caring, and wholesome home was provided by his godmother, Cheryl Yellowfawn Scott.

She lived in Mount Airy, North Carolina, and was a major influence in his life, especially during his formative years.

She and his mother had developed a close bond during their university years. After graduation, they maintained a friendship that grew throughout their lives like a well-watered garden.

When a bundle of joy came on the scene, it was only natural to ask Cheryl to be the godparent and guardian while mom was commissioned.

Her enlightened mind and active lifestyle added

richness to the growth and development of Jonathan. Her community leadership and kind thoughtfulness had a tremendous impact on the man he became. It all helped shape his character and cultivate his kindness

Sometimes he would be in Mount Airy for months before going back home to be with his mom as she returned from her naval duty.

He fondly recalled youthful times with his godmother, "I remember the delightful warm summer days playing outside, the cold winter fun we had snow sledding down the hills, and most of all, I remember the kindness found in a small town."

His body gently shook as he chuckled, "During the times I lived with her, I was raised by almost everyone in the church we attended."

The quality time he spent with her included visits from her to where mother and son were based. He remembers living on the post in New Jersey and she came to celebrate his birthday. He was four years old. Yet, the memory was chiseled skillfully on the slate of favorite memories.

Cheryl and her sister LaDonna came with plans to take him to see Cats on Broadway. It was an intentional memory-making gift. He recalls similar kindness generously given throughout his life. All of them added to the treasure chest of lasting memories.

While talking about the play, he reminiscences, "Everything was dark, and the actors dressed like cats started walking all around. The aisles were filled with glowing eyes. To be honest, a four-year-old was terrified." Nonetheless, all the costumes, the stairway on stage, and the heaven scene engraved images in his mind. He said, "I remember, it was all so cool. No, doubt this experience gave me a love for theatre."

Thinking back, he acknowledged the many generous acts of kindness that helped shape the direction his life would take. They helped him develop a philosophy of kindness that continues to guide his life.

Pausing briefly, after he shared the memory, he recalled an earlier thoughtful deed that had fastened to his memory. He was three years old, but in his recollection, it was as real as a movie trailer.

He and his mom were in a restaurant. As he was trained, he sat quietly and politely waiting for the food to be served. The lady sitting behind them got up to leave and walked to their table and apologized. She shared that she was a little aggravated to be sat at a table by a small child. She expected the tot to be loud, fretful, and disturb the patrons but to her surprise, he sat like a perfect little gentleman. In appreciation for politeness, she paid for their meal. This impressionable experience along with other influencing memories flow like little streams through his mind

It was at the age of seven when permanent roots were planted. Now that his mom was retiring, the small family could settle down to live in one location. They could remain near the base in New Jersey, move to DC, or any of the other many places they had visited or lived.

Unsurprisingly, when she asked where he wanted to live, he knew it was Mount Airy. His chosen forever home was familiar and filled with fond memories. With a permanent home, the first grader started school in Mount Airy.

Kindness, like a familiar garment, clothed his childhood and draped his youth. His mom faithfully modeled kindness. He said, when he was a little kid, he did not always understand that the many benevolent things she did by helping other people were "kindness". Looking back, he understands kindness has always been a part of his family.

One of the family traditions began 23 years ago. Each Thanksgiving, he, his family, and friends, along with many other volunteers go to a local church and distribute food. With insight, he said, "The older I get the more I realize all those people helping are being kind." Melva Houston, a local famous jazz singer, and organizer of the event would always be there and ride with them to deliver the meals. (see Appendix II More on MAin...Melva's Alley and More Murals)

The annual event serves over 400 people. It is a community effort with local restaurants, scouts, churches, and neighbors helping neighbors. He noted the small Mount Airy community has many active organizations that help with kindness to meet the needs of the neighbors in our small town.

His church provided more opportunities for good deeds. They organized visits to local nursing homes to sing to the older residents. While there, he noticed some had no family or friends who visited. Moved with kindness, he went back to visit them. To this day, he continues to visit them as friends.

"I recall many of my teachers were kind as well." He affirmed. Recalling Debbie Severs Diamont, one of his teachers, he said she demonstrated the kindness of inclusion as she strove to involve all students. (see Appendix IV - Famous People from Mount Airy)

Mr. Stone, his Spanish teacher, is another mentor who shrouded him in kindness. "One of the benefits of living in a small town is so many of us have these shared memorable experiences, and in turn, we share the kindness with each other."

He continued. Describing another teacher, Robert Hill, he said, "He and his family are the kindest people I have ever met." He trumpeted, "To this day, they make me feel like family." (see Appendix III Beyond MAin...Mount Airy City Schools)

After graduating from the local high school, he moved to attend UNC Pembroke. While working on his degree in theatre, he developed friendships that were authentic and meaningful. With confidence, he stated, "My good university friends are the type of people that will give you the shirt off their back." As friends, they went through things together and stuck together like a family. They sat together to study, helped each other when in trouble, and even bought meals for each other when money was tight.

"I remember," he said with warm comfort, "the Resident Assistant of our dorm. He came to check on me after the death of my godmother's mom. The kindness of checking on a mourning friend in a time of need impacted my life forever. He didn't have to do it, but he did."

Continuing to recall kind mentors, he spoke about Debbie Cochran and his interning at one of the local historic radio stations. "When I started," he said, "she was the mayor, and one of the DJs. You do not always remember what people say, but you always remember how they made you feel." He said, "Her kindness is etched in my mind." (see Appendix III Beyond MAin...Historic Radio Stations)

To those that know him, Jonathan is thoughtful and has a kind and gentle character. He is known for helping.

He began volunteering at the Mount Airy Regional Museum of History. They found him to be considerate and reliable and eventually employed him. He thoroughly enjoys greeting customers, setting up displays, and helping with the Junior Historians. (see Appendix II More on MAin...Mount Airy Museum of Regional History)

As time goes on, he finds more time is spent helping his mom. He feels his numerous experiences interacting in kindness with others aid him in being a kind and caring support for her as she begins to need small assistance.

His life experiences and observations formed his perspective, he noted. "It is always better to be nice, if you are nice, for the most part, people are nice back. I had rather be remembered for doing something nice rather than be remembered for being unkind."

His daily goal is to make one person smile. "If I do that," he said in satisfaction, "I have done something good. I will have left the world a bit brighter."

Before our conversation ended, Ray a local homeless man was mentioned. Ray has housing but because of intellectual disabilities, he prefers hanging out on the streets and can be seen in local businesses. Jonathan said, "People downtown talk to him, and we make sure he is okay. Occasionally, I or others bring him lunch and a drink. I make it a point to talk to him." Sometimes acknowledging someone is the kindest thing you can do. Human touch and interaction are kindness.

He concluded by saying. "All you have to do is open a door for someone, give them a smile. Say thank you for the little things. When someone speaks, speak back with gentleness. I think most everyone is nice, they just forget sometimes to be kind."

Kindness is contagious.

Our small town has some of the kindest people you will ever meet.

Calvin B. Vaughn, Jr.

Jonathan Lightfoot at the Mount Airy Regional Museum of History's entrance, featuring Pilot Mountain

Laughter...Paul McCraw

His laughter was full of life as he recounted the story, he had told 100 times. His hearty chuckle bellowed as fresh as it roared 73 years ago when then, the 13-year-old's guffaws echoed through the meadows of the Red Brush community. (see Appendix III Beyond MAin...Communities and Towns in Surry County).

Covering his face with a smile, he recalled. "I was tickled beyond belief, I even bent over laughing at what happened to my brother." His brother had gone fishing with a homemade rod and reel. The boy's faithful hound dog trotted behind him. As he cast the simplistic rod into the river, it caught in the dog's ear. The baying hound took off like a slingshot, dragging the reel, his brother running behind. Recalling the story again caused Paul to burst into laughter.

Enjoying a leisurely lunch and cheerful conversation at Barney's Cafe, Paul McCraw was brimming with jubilation. His laugh was genuine, amusing, and contagious. He was full of spirit and filled with joy. If he were not already a friend, the laughter that sprinkled our conversation with merriment would have drawn me into fellowship with him. (see Appendix II More on MAin...Restaurants Downtown)

Yet, while reflecting on his life, his gentle laugh was temporarily muffled by an emotion of sadness. "I've been pretty happy all my life. The hardest thing is getting over the loss of my wife."

Quoting the date of her passing, he said they were married 61 years and almost 4 months. "Hazel was a good woman. She was tough too. She had to be tough to put up with me." He gently chuckled.

Hazel Griffith, the youngest daughter of Andy Griffith's uncle, grew up only ½ mile from Andy's homeplace. Her dad ran a small community store, and her family lived beside the store.

After marrying Paul, she moved a few houses down the street. The same street where she lived her entire life. Happily, with her husband, she raised her only son in the same house.

Today, the house is full of wonderful memories and sits downhill, in perfect view of the giant sky-blue water tower with the bigger-than-life size Andy Griffith and Opie going fishing image. The water tower is located on the street her cousin, Andy Griffith, grew up on, and is a welcome beacon to anyone entering Mount Airy from Rockford Street. (see Appendix III Beyond MAin...Andy Griffith Homeplace)

His wife, Hazel, played the piano. She started playing when she was 12. She played at the same church most of her life. Interestingly, the pianist on the Andy Griffith Show was named Hazel. She too, always played for the church choir. Paul said, "My Hazel played the piano for the church until she was 75 years old." Smiling, he crooned, "Huuuum."

Grinning with an insider's point of view, Paul stated, "You know Andy wanted to make out like he didn't make the show after Mount Airy, but there are too many coincidences." (see Appendix II More on MAin...Is Mount Airy, Mayberry?)

As his face remained lit with merriment, Paul continued sharing stories about Andy. "You know he came to town more than people think, he stayed out of sight, and sometimes stayed on the mountain, up near Galax, Virginia."

When Andy first experienced financial success, he came to town for a visit. Paul asked him, "What are you going to do with all that money?" Andy answered, "I am going to pay off my debt and buy daddy a gold pocket watch."

Many years later, when Andy came into town for the dedication of the Andy Griffith Parkway, the Griffith family had gathered at a cousin's house. Wondering about the watch, Paul asked him a question, "Andy, what did you do with that watch you bought your dad?" Reaching in his pocket, with the all-familiar Andy smile, he pulled out the pocket watch and showed it off like a prized possession.

He recalls the unassuming movie star did not make a big splash when he came to town. The only flashy time he remembers is in 1958. Andy had already been nominated for a Tony for his Broadway role in *No Time for Sergeants* and his film debut in *A Face in the Crowd* had just been released. Paul chortled as he spoke, "He rolled into town driving a sparkling new 58' loaded convertible Thunderbird."

Parked in front of the modest Griffith home, scores of people flocked to see him, hovering around the polished car that mirrored their gawking faces. It created a lot of hooplas and unwanted attention.

Paul chuckled as he remembered the next time Andy drove into town. He pulled up to his cousin's home and stopped. Paul and Hazel peered through the curtain. The first thing they saw was an old rusted-out 1955 station wagon. Looking more closely, they recognized Andy, and his two children sitting in the back.

The new disguise worked; few people noticed the successful TV star was in his hometown. He said by this time Andy was a big star traveling all over the country and living in Los Angeles. (see Appendix III Beyond MAin...Andy Griffith)

Paul has traveled beyond Mount Airy as well. His military service took him to other states and stationed him in Alabama. Vacations were times for travel as well. He enjoyed an extended vacation when he and Hazel explored the western part of our country. His biggest trip was a pilgrimage to Israel, yet he loves Mount Airy the most.

"I have traveled some, but I love living in this town! It has been good for me. I have been living in the city limits for more than 60 years. It is a great city with great city services." He stated with firm belief.

Reminiscing, Paul continued. "I have always had good health. For most of my life, I have been blessed." As any good storyteller can, he artistically chronicled his life, sprinkling it with laughter, commemorating his good friends, and thinking back on all the good times. Intently listening, I had a wide smile.

His 86-year-old mind is sharp as a tack. He spits out dates like he is counting to ten or quoting the ABCs. He knows the year for most events in his life and, often, the month and date.

His advice for life and laughter is simple. Along with many who live in the bible belt, he professes, "The main thing is to live for the Lord and be kind to people."

He testified that his faith was brought to life at an old-fashioned Brush Arbor Meeting. With a glowing smile and gentle mirth, he shared his faith. "I'm so old I remember church meetings in a grove." At the age of five, the little boy sat on a log, looked up at the sky, surrounded by trees, and found faith. He recalls, the community of believers worshipped outside until a church could be built. Today, with mature faith, he teaches Sunday School at a church near his home.

He shared how he valued growing up in the country. Recalling his youthful days living on the farm, he remembers his family taught him good morals, respect, honesty, and hard work. With pride, he served two years in the Army, which he said taught him more respect.

As soon as his service time was over, he moved into town. He had one vocation after the service. He worked as a fixer in the local hosiery mills. Suppressing a manly giggle, as his body shook with joviality, he said, "Sometimes I think we tore up more than we fixed."

During his career in the textile mills, he had a great time building relationships. By always joking around, and having fun, he brought connection through laughter into the workplace. He remembers always being surrounded by friends, laughing in harmony.

He created big smiles on the faces of most co-workers. Remembering one smiling face in particular, who responded to his jesting, he recalls him saying, "You ain't right." With hearty laughter, Paul continued, "I have been told that a lot of times." And he laughed again.

"We can do some foolish things, but life is good, and we always need to laugh. He further stated, with pearls of glee. "I've always heard, the Good Lord looks after fools and babies and I ain't no baby."

Join Paul and many others in our small town who have learned to laugh.

Proverbs 17:21 A merry heart does good like a medicine.

Paul McGraw
Andy Griffith's Cousin
with the Andy Griffith Water Tower in the Background

Loyalty...Mark Gillespie

Dark clouds lay silent on Main Street. The heavens sprinkled tears. The downtown bustle paused as silence subdued the usual noise. Mourning souls stood like statues. Somber heads bowed as the procession rolled by.

The business community and friends respectfully lined the sidewalks as the olive-green hearse ferrying the body of blues, and gospel singer, Melva Houston slowly passed. A recording of her world-famous voice permeated the streets as the jazzy lonesome sound flowed from speakers hanging at the corner of each block. She was one of our own, and it is our tradition, as the parade of mourners drives by, we stand in respect for our friends. (see Appendix II More on MAin...Melva's Alley and other Murals)

Mark Gillespie tearfully drove, as we followed the cortege. Sitting on the passenger's side, I looked to the right and saw all the people gathered along the street, then I turned to my friend at the wheel. Moved with emotion, he said, "She was a loyal friend." For 40 years, they had been faithful friends.

Loyalty is something he knows about and values very much.

Often visiting him, I witness the procession of loyal friends dropping by his home. Like an endless parade, they visit on regular schedules. Others phone like clockwork. Many are childhood buddies; many are school friends.

On one occasion, I shared my admiration for the allegiance of his faithful friends. He said, "Everybody is worth knowing because you learn something from everyone you meet, good or bad, just throw the bad away, and keep the good." No doubt, the value he sees in each person allows lifelong attachments.

Our many conversations revealed his broader circle of

acquaintances. He knew some of the most interesting people in Surry County, and the world, and he knew their colorful stories. I was intrigued, but I wanted to know more about his prismatic life.

No less interesting is his family. His mother, from South Carolina, portrays all that is grand about southern belles, she is full of grace. His dad, a businessman, and his family from North Carolina, demonstrated the success of the American dream, through hard work.

Mark's well-connected southern parents created for him a captivating childhood. For the first 13 years of his life, he lived in Central and South America. His father worked for the British Tobacco Company, teaching rural Latin communities how to farm. Mark was born in the largest central American republic, Nicaragua. After his birth, the family lived in Columbia, Venezuela, El Salvador, Honduras, and Costa Rica.

Mark Gillespie

Sheltered from the woes of poor economics in developing countries, he lived a privileged life. On foreign soil, he enjoyed the luxuries afforded to a successful American busi

Comfortably settled in the large fi front of the plane, or the best suite on the ship was a normal way to travel. Like the scene from the first-class passengers boarding the Titanic, he remembers the family taking 26 pieces of luggage on one cruise.

His Latin years were spent in opulent housing cocooned inside a compound. It was supplied by the company. He remembers bars on the windows and security guards. It was a protected country club life with swimming pools, cocktail parties, and abundance.

He and his closest companions, his two sisters, enjoyed

the comfort of maids, gardeners, and nannies. Dinner guests were ambassadors, dignitaries, and presidents. He recalls it being the "good life".

As a child, he moved six times, forcing him to leave his boyhood friends. Although challenging, he quickly learned to develop close relationships. Never forgetting his friendships, he learned to value them. The constant change allowed him to become skilled in making new friends with everyone.

At a very young age, he began to feel compassion. He recalls one of his earliest humanitarian emotions, which he feels, birthed the compassion that influenced his future. Thinking back, he said the feelings he experienced when he first saw people without what he had guided his life's direction, resulting in an educational path that led to a career in service.

Reflecting on a mental snapshot, he described seeing people lined up in front of the compound gate. They had buckets on their heads. Some were carrying water pots. The guards, which protected him, held a water hose, as they sprayed water to fill their vessels. Something about the scene broke the tender heart of the young boy. From that time on, he knew he wanted to do something to help other people.

Another early life memory further guided his altruistic path. It was the first time, at age six, he traveled with his dad outside the gated community. In a Jeep, bumping over dusty dirt roads they went to a remote area.

They stopped at a little stucco and mud house with a shabby store attached. Spending the night, their accommodations were quite simple. In unfamiliar surroundings, Mark's eyes peered through the smudged windows, at the stray dogs scampering through the bobbed wire fences. The food and table setting were meager. But the hospitality of baking, just for him, a fresh pineapple cake was something a wide-eyed child never forgot.

These people reminded him of the thirsty people who lined up for water at the compound. Becoming more aware, he began to see others lived vastly differently from his favored life. His youthful mind formed deep thoughts, "How do they live like this?" As an adult, he would construct a mature response. "I can help." And he did.

Civil unrest in El Salvador and his dad's health issue caused the family to move to Beulah, North Carolina, about 12 miles west of Mount Airy. The teenager found himself living in a rural unincorporated community in Surry County on HWY 89, bordering Virginia

The move from an affluent compound to living on a 350-acre working farm was life-changing for the boy with the silver spoon in his mouth. "I hated becoming a *farm boy*." He declared. Assimilating to the southern farm life was a daunting challenge. The transition was like going from a pristine swimming pool to a muddy creek.

"I felt like I had gone from riches to rags. For me, the grass was not greener on the farm. I know rich and I know a hard farm life and rich is much better!" He proclaimed. For him, the difficult life of a farm boy was an insurmountable struggle.

Just a few days after moving onto the farm, his dad called for him. With anticipation, he trotted to the barn. To his surprise, he gazed at a local man hand-milking a cow. His dad spoke to the man, "I want you to teach Mark how to milk." Mark's neck turned so fast; he felt a sharp streak of pain. Horrified, he glared at the rough hands squeezing the tits, he heard the squirt of the milk hitting the pale. Without another thought, he spun around and ran as fast as he could back to the house.

Although repulsed by country living, he learned to farm. He primed tobacco. He mended fences. He watered and fed the cattle and gathered up hay. He worked ridiculously hard as a farm boy, but he never milked a cow. Some lines he would not cross.

His newly learned farming skills and toiling labor throughout his teen years gave him a high respect for farmers and cattlemen. He extolled, "They are to be commended for all they do."

As his admiration for hard work grew so did his disgust as a farm boy.

He began to plot his escape. "How can I get out of farming for the rest of my life? He fretted. With less than model grades, education did not appear to be the solution, until his dad gave some motivational advice, "If you don't straighten out your grades, you will be stuck on the farm for the rest of your life."

The freedom-seeking student with questionable grades began to focus on education. He had a plan to flee the farm. Motivated on his path to liberation, higher education allowed his escape.

He was granted admittance into Wingate College. He noted modest improvement in grades helped but acknowledged family connections are always more beneficial. In college, he was committed, and he made the dean's list.

Initially, the newfound liberty proved to be lonesome. With all his friends at other universities and his family back on the farm, it was the first time he was alone. Strong-willed, he managed his feelings. Sister Sledge's singing, *We Are Family,* inspired him and became his daily companion.

The loneliness provided an opportunity to make more loyal friends. During his college years, he forged friendships that last a lifetime. His natural ability to bond aided in banking a reserve of loyal friends.

The late 70s hold the best memories for him. It was a "coming of age". The disco music, the social life, and new adventures richly adorned the life of the former farm boy. The time of enlightenment coupled with his compassionate heart provided clear direction for his future.

His love for helping people expanded to politics. He

loves politics. He understands it is a path to make positive changes. His active political life began as a State Senate Page.

He knew he wanted to make a difference. From the first time he saw poverty in Central America, his desire to help others grew. Now that he was off the farm, the young, educated man, with a master's in human development, began to live life independently in the big city. He recalls it was a grand time.

After the good life in the Queen City (Charlotte), he moved back to Surry County and began working at Crossroads Behavioral Health. The experience was life-changing for the certified counselor. He had discovered his calling. He said, "I had a career, not a job." Each life event allowed him to journey further on his humanitarian path.

After working with Mount Airy's developmentally disabled, he transferred to Piedmont Mental Health, serving three counties. Next, he returned to Charlotte to continue his career in mental health, and eventually, he had his own practice. Due to an MS diagnosis, he completed his career and retired.

If you know Mark, you know he was born to taste the finer things in life. He appreciates sophistication. Class and elegance are attracted to him. However, looking back, he feels his greatest wealth is the privilege to have lived a life filled with amazing and abundant experiences.

His travels across America polished his savoir-vivre. Cruising the Caribbean increased his diverse cultural appetite. Socializing with numerous Miss Americas elevated his style. Political conversations with the Clintons, Al Gore, and Governor Dukakis widened his worldview.

Meeting superstars, for example, Dolly, Diana Ross, Arnold Palmer, Richard Burton, and Melva Houston enriched his life. Partying with Donald Trump (long before he ran for office), and Marla Maples connected him to the rich and famous. But his treasure lies in his amassment of loyal friends.

The socialite shared his view on loyalty. Wisely, he stated, "A loyal person will stand with you, no matter if you are right or wrong. They will let you know if you are wrong, but they stand behind you."

His elegant mom, with solid Christian values, is one of the first persons he mentions when talking about loyal people. He says she is as dependable as a rock. She is always giving and constantly shows support.

He has high regard for another person who demonstrated allegiance as a loyal friend. He was an influential teacher, Sandy Beam. The music teacher was a role model and proved that real men can be gentle kind and artsy. He provided intellectual conversation that led to deep philosophical thought. His classroom was a safe harbor for troubled youth, especially a young farm boy who needed a life source.

After retiring from education, his friend, the teacher developed *Voce*, a choral ensemble made up of locals (many former students). The ensemble performs choral literature from all the major style periods. They provide outstanding local concerts. Music professionals, and extensively trained vocalists, along with those who love singing make up the group. When Mr. Beam died, his loyal students repaid him by sustaining his legacy. The group remains active. As a loyal friend, Mark is instrumental in its preservation. (See Appendix III Beyond MAin – Community Large Singing Groups

Loyalty is difficult to define, yet it is easily seen in the faithfulness of friends. The bond Mark has developed with his lifelong friends is both heartwarming and inspiring.

It is a blessing to have such a large circle of committed friends who never let go. Friends from his childhood, school days, and career arrive on schedule, like a slow-moving train chugging along, parading through his home.

He said, "If I go tomorrow, I've had a good time, I have

scarred, and I've been scarred. Life is sad and life is happy but loyal family and friends make anything better."

The song playing on the speakers, as we rode in the funeral parade was *Come Sunday* recorded on Melva Houston's Black Coffee CD and written by Duke Ellington. It is a story about the assuredness that everything will be all right. Regardless of how dark it gets; you can always count on Sunday's relief.

If you want the riches of loyalty - be loyal. You can be somebody's "Sunday relief". Loyal friends make everything all right.

Our small town is seasoned with loyal friends.

Melva Houston
A Loyal Friend, Jazz, Blues, and Gospel Singer

Neighborly Love...The Rees Family

Presbyterian minister, Fred Rogers, created *Mister Roger's Neighborhood,* a children's television series that teaches how to be thoughtful, loving, and caring neighbors. He said, "Deep within us – no matter who we are – there lives a feeling of wanting to be loveable...and the greatest thing we can do is to let people know that they are loved and capable of loving."

Love is not only a feeling, but love can be seen in action. When love is experienced only as a feeling it can be limiting, when love is expressed in action, it can be seen in endless good deeds to others.

The phrase, "I love you," also conveys different levels of meaning, it depends on the target of our expression. For example, the meaning of the proclamation of love to family members, friends, and partners is vastly differ

Calvin "the Red Hat Guy"

The verbal declaration of love is pleasing to hear but just hearing or only feeling love does not necessarily help us when we have basic needs, but neighborly love (which shows action) does. Acts of kindness are demonstrations of neighborly love; these acts exhibit the fullness of love.

Our faith teaches us to love our neighbor as we love ourselves. Our neighbor is anyone we encounter during our daily routine. In times when acts of love are seldom seen, the question must be asked, "How do we increase acts of love in our community that make it beneficial to our neighbor." I think the answer is found within the character of small towns across America.

Friendly folk, who are kind, and giving have always been visible in small-town America. Mount Airy, especially, has always been an affable little town. It is a place where neighborly love is not only seen but cherished.

In Mount Airy's yesteryear, people were seen gathering off Main Street, along West Oak Street while others shopped. The "spot" was a place to whittle, chew tobacco, swap stories, and practice being neighborly. Today, the *Whittling Wall* (outdoor art wall) located along the street recognizes some of our local citizens who have contributed to the community. (see Appendix II More on MAin...Whittling Wall)

One of those honored on the Wall is Floyd E. (Flip) Rees. He operated one of the best clothing shops in town which opened in 1946, and the store continues in operation today at 198 North Main Street.

The quality of clothing and the high level of service drew customers from every socioeconomic level. It has always drawn upscale shoppers as well as budget-conscious shoppers looking for finery. In the past, farmers and mill workers saved for months to buy that one-of-a-kind dress or that Sunday best "outfit" from the Main Street shop.

Main Street is another gathering place for neighbors. Usually, on Saturdays, many working people would get up early, do the chores and have breakfast at the table with a loving family.

The table was set with piles of bacon, slabs of ham, free-range eggs, country gravy, and handmade biscuits, while apple butter and jams filled the table. The routine was always the same, get up, wash up, and get dressed up, followed by the weekly trip "to go uptown".

Uptown was the spot to be. Loads of people could be found in the hardware store and in the dime store. The streets bubbled with activity. Folks treated themselves at the soda fountain. Aliments were cured at the apothecaries. In the shoe repair or barber shop, men would prattle. In some dress shops, ladies had dresses made with cut cloth. In others, like Rees Clothing Co., fine clothing was purchased.

For many in the hollows of Surry County, clothes were not bought to be crammed into crowded closets. They were sparingly purchased for a specific purpose. Usually, a special occasion was in mind. For some, the procurement was the only fall or spring attire purchased.

After the sale was made, at home in just the right place, the clothing would hang in the wardrobe. With delight, they could point to it and say "That is my special outfit. I am going to wear it Saturday night."

When Saturday night came, they put on the rarely bought store garment and they felt different, important, and special. As they swaggered among friends, you might hear someone give them a good-hearted compliment, "You are uptown tonight." It would make them smile and feel valued.

Being complimentary is one way that neighborly love is shown. Intentional compliments require little effort. They contain powerful words. Merely hearing complimentary words, elevates your self-image. You may have worked hard, sweated, had dirty hands, and eaten beans, and fried "taters" for dinner but the recognition made you feel good. Maybe you had little money in your pocket but feeling "uptown" made you feel royal.

Far too many people feel less than royal. They feel unimportant, unnoticed, and less than. In life, people have hurts, disappointments, and put-downs. Unkind words cause people to struggle as they look for happiness. But you and I can lift people as we demonstrate neighborly love.

Everyone, regardless of how little you have or how

much you have, each person can take the time to make someone feel better by giving others a flattering remark. There are limitless ways to show love through kind words. You can share neighborly love by becoming a complimentary person.

If you are accomplished or a successful businessperson, you can impart kindness and help make someone's day special. If you are living the life of "uptown", you can share some "uptown" kindness with neighborly love. In a position of success and favor you are uniquely positioned to help make someone's life a little better.

Flip Rees, a successful businessman provided a great example of someone who extended kindness to the community. He passed in 2009, but he had a lasting impact on Mount Airy.

He knew that some of his patrons were farmers who relied on the fall harvest for earnings. He knew others were mill workers, who might need a line of credit. He allowed customers to pay a little each week or when they could. Everyone was treated the same. He showed kindness and love.

Rees was a gentleman and became an icon in our town. His neighborly kindness goes far beyond what he had done for individuals; there are not many charitable activities that he did not support. He was instrumental in the start of today's successful downtown revitalization, and he was vital in the formation of Surry Community College.

Today, his family and the sales staff continue the tradition of demonstrating neighborly love. Susan, Flip's only daughter, is deceased. She was known for community service. Her legacy mirrors her dad's. Both sons, Gene, and John are active in the community and are outstanding citizens. The entire family has demonstrated what loving your neighbor looks like.

All of us, in our day-to-day journey, can take a moment and notice our neighbor. Neighbors are more than the people who live next door, they are all around us, the people who cross our paths each day. The people you see on Main Street.

With little effort and heartful intention, you can be neighborly.

You may not own a business, but you can speak uplifting words. You can give a compliment about someone's smile, recognize, and speak a thoughtful word about their kind act or say something nice about their new hairstyle. Mention the cuteness of their child and flatter them by pointing out their special attire. Praise them for their contagious laughter. With a little bit of thought, you can perform a simple act of love with a compliment. A small gesture makes anyone feel better.

It is simple. Everyone can make a difference in someone's life. Be intentional and keep the heart of small-town America alive by lavishly showering others with neighborly love.

Neighborly love built our small town.

Randy Collins, Mount Airy Chamber President visiting F. Rees Clothing Store

Optimism...The Montalvos

Huddled alone in the bathroom, the overwhelming fear gripped her, it would not let go. Panic pierced her soul, she was smothering.

Her rapid breath was packed with prayer. Petitions were as relentless as the pounding rain.

The wind traveling 175 MPH screeched like a roaring train. The violent vibrations intensified; the building rumbled, ready to shatter like a fragile box. The 60-mile-wide hurricane was a direct hit on the 35-mile-wide island. Nearly a category 5, Hurricane Maria was the worst storm to hit the island in more than 80 years. Puerto Rico was wreaked, in the final count, 2,975 islanders would be dead.

It was Wednesday, September 20, 2017, when Lillian, frozen in fear, thought she was going to die. She had never faced anything as frightening. With sobering conviction, she said, "I knew I could not control what was happening to me." The fierce storm tried to rob her of optimism.

In the middle of the five-hour horrific experience, she recalled words of faith.

"Be still and know that I am Lord."

During the crisis, she remembered the story of how Jesus calmed the sea when the disciples panicked. While the storm howled, she said to herself, "If you believe God's message of faith, then this is the time to surrender." Miraculously, she felt a numbing calmness and she knew everything would be okay." Through it all, her faith was strengthened, and her optimism grew.

Nelson, her husband is also an optimist. Ironically, he has experienced a lot of hurricanes.

His experiences with storms are a little different. He served as an autopilot instrument technician with the "Hurricane Hunters Unit" for the United States Air Force.

His job, along with the team, was to fly directly into the eye of storms. On each hunt, the specially equipped aircraft plowed through the winds and the rains, and he remained calm each time. He trusted the controls. He was confident. Although tested, his optimism grew stronger.

The Airman had a full-service career for our country. Much of his service time included the Vietnam War Era.

For many, the conflict was devastating. The families suffered from heartbreak as their loved ones came home maimed and broken and some came home in boxes. The scale of fighting, for that war, was enormous. The human cost was colossal, over 58,000 American servicemen and women died, and over 1,500 remain missing.

Although there was never a declaration of war, and the exact dates are debatable, the Vietnam War lasted for about 20 years. The soldiers would see things that caused nightmares. The mutilation of bodies and the vast number of young soldiers stacked in green body bags was unimaginable. No human should ever have to see the horror, brutality, and deprivation witnessed by these men and women.

Mount Airy's Veterans' Memorial

The soldiers who lost their lives were shipped home. It was a daily tragedy.

Firsthand, Nelson watched the steady stream of death swell with the youthful bodies flowing home. He said, "I felt helpless and angered at the destruction of human lives." He lamented with deep emotion, "I still get choked up thinking about it."

Day after day, month after month, he saw the deluge of death stream from foreign soil. The front-row seat to the human carnage and needless slaughter wore on his soul. The darkness of constant death tried to destroy his hope. The decimation would make some men lose their faith, but not Nelson, he refused to let go.

His faith, the strength of his mother, childhood influencers, and the support of Lillian enabled him to remain an optimistic person. He learned to practice the skill of optimism.

You may be born with a seed of optimism, but optimism is a skill that you must learn to practice, much like learning to play an instrument. Lillian said, "I believe, my glass-half-full attitude is part innate, and partly learned from family, school, friends, and culture." Nelson agrees, he said, "I have always looked for good. My influencers are my mom, the neighborhood grocer, early jobs, college and the air force, all contributed to my positive outlook."

Sparked in their childhood, and built over their lifetime, the Montalvos have become resilient through optimism. They are emotionally healthy, and content in life by developing the skill of optimism. They always see their glass half full (if not overflowing with blessings).

Several life-altering events in each of their lives made them who they are today. In each life event, they looked for lessons. They learned from each of the challenges. They developed skills that helped them be positive overcomers.

The seeds of Lillian's success can be traced to the dreams of her parents. Being blue-collar laborers, they had aspirations that their little girl would have a better life.

In her formative years, the influence of her "village" helped her develop a positive outlook. In the first grade, she had learning challenges that tried to dampen her parents' dream, but with support and budding hope, she overcame them.

By the seventh grade, she was excelling and was awarded academic honors. After receiving one award, she thanked a Sister in the parochial school for the medal. The Sister responded, "No, you thank yourself."

The words sparked a drive in her pursuit of optimism. Speaking to herself, she said. "I realized then that only I can make my destiny." She began to read books about the power of shaping your thoughts and she began to absorb the positive talk from people like Oprah. With determination, her optimism began to mature.

Little did she know, she was preparing herself to face a colossal trial. A health scare tested her and tried to squelch her hopeful faith. At the age of 19, she was diagnosed with malignant melanoma. Facing the journey with hope, once again, she overcame.

The crisis taught her two things. First, triumphing over the near-death illness taught her to be more thankful, and second, the experience gave her an understanding of others who walk the path of cancer. She became a person living in gratitude and she became a woman of prayer. With a thankful heart, she utters regular prayers for cancer patients.

Her optimism grew stronger. The little girl from humble beginnings, who overcame insurmountable challenges, went on to earn two college degrees and become a certified School Psychologist.

Nelson, also, overcame struggles in life and became a respected and successful man who views life with optimism.

The seeds of his optimism and success were sown by his mother Carmen and watered by mentors.

His mom was open-minded, loving, giving, and strict but a fair woman. He said, "She taught me to be responsible, strong, and a compassionate man." Even though she is passed, with a heart of love, he said, "I still shed tears of love for her."

Building on this solid family foundation, and encouraged by others, he earned a Bachelor of Fine Arts degree, worked as a successful freelance photographer and he had an exemplary air force career. His accomplishments have been recognized with scholarships and national honors.

The Montalvos attribute the materialization of their dreams and the manifestation of their successes to optimistic faith. Looking back, they identify contributing factors that matured their faith and built a positive outlook on life.

First, they acknowledge the support of friends and family. Next, they built on optimism through visualization, planning, persistence, relentlessness, hard work, perspiration, inspiration, prayers, and an unexplained inner drive.

I agree with them. Optimism is planted like a seed in each of us at birth. However, the seed must grow. Optimism is a valuable skill to be cultivated.

Just like this caring couple, life will throw devastating things at you, but optimism will help you overcome them.

Optimists develop the "skill" to see differently. Optimists plan for success, overcome challenges, and draw from inner strength to say, "Yes, we can."

Since, my senior year in high school, I have stood on a truth that one of my heroes, Frances Draughn, shared with me. *See the chapter on Friends for more about Ms. Draughn.* As a graduation gift, she gave me a bible. These words were written on the inside: *"We can be sure that "all" things work together for our good, if we have faith and love God."*

From the influence of strong mentors, I have learned to live with confidence, God orchestrates everything to work toward something good and beautiful when I love Him and accept His invitation to live according to His plan. This amazing truth enabled me to develop the skill of optimism.

Just like the Montalvos, I see life half full, if not overflowing.

Both, Lillian, and Nelson are amazing people. Over time, we have become close friends. Recently, they visited me in Mount Airy. I toured them around town. We visited the Mount Airy Regional Museum of History, along with other interesting sites. They loved it. (see Appendix II More on MAin...Mount Airy Museum of Regional History)

The couple not only loved the museum, but they fell in love with the serenity and friendliness found in our small town. They were surprised to see there is so much to do and experience in Mount Airy. They especially like the lively and positive vibe they felt while downtown. (see Appendix I Things to do in Mount Airy)

Although they have a home in High Point, NC, and a home in Puerto Rico, they bought a home in Mount Airy, so they can spend more time here. They are from New York, lived in California, and are Puerto Rican descent but they love the values and charm of small-town America.

Their hearts are filled with goodness. It is the good-hearted people that make Mount Airy a great place to live. And the Montalvos fit perfectly into our community.

Our small town is filled with good people like them. Some were born here, and others, from all over the country, have chosen to live here.

Nelson, Lillian, and Calvin
at the Rockford General Store, Historic Rockford, NC

Push…Christopher Stolz

Dangling from the door of the helicopter, he pushed himself out. Focused, he used his strength to prevent the swaying. The last thing you want, while suspended from a helicopter, is to flop around like a rag doll and drop your camera.

Mission accomplished. Suspended from the metal bird, the photographer captured the storytelling image on film.

Christopher Stolz is a photographer with experience in combat photography. His career spans the globe, from Guantanamo Bay, Cuba, to Baghdad, Iraq, and to Tokyo, Japan. In five of his 14 years of service, he worked from a helicopter as an aerial photographer for the USS Harry S. Truman.

He wanted to join the navy after he graduated from Mount Airy High School. As a volunteer recruitment, he had options. He chose the field of military photography.

He was assigned to the public affairs division, and he was taken under the wings of experienced photographers. They often sat together and talked about what makes a good photograph. Feasting from their buffet of knowledge, he soaked in all their wisdom and learned from their experiences.

While in service, the shutter on his camera would open and close thousands of times, catching the images, from a lone soldier to an aerial view of an enormous carrier. During those years, he sharpened his ability to take photographs and process film.

After a few years, the military photographer grew restless. His thirst to increase the skills of his craft intensified. He felt he could do more.

A once-in-a-lifetime opportunity came knocking in 2004, he was one of only five U.S. Navy still photographers selected to study advanced photojournalism at the Newhouse School of Public Communication at Syracuse University. It was a unique chance to polish his craft. He took advantage of the favorable moment and satisfied his craving for more knowledge.

Like a dry sponge in a bucket of water, he soaked in all he could from the professors. His respect (he had developed in his youth) for teachers gave him a keen ability to listen to them. He had an overwhelming hunger to learn from his educators.

He expanded his knowledge about photojournalism. He studied design elements and visual communication and he acquired the ability to craft photos. His skills noticeably improved.

The professional training increased and grew his confidence as an artist. As his artistic ability continued to mature, he improved his craft of storytelling with photography. Taking photographs became much more than snapping a shot, it became a process of creating art that revealed a story. He embraced the belief that his elevated artistic skill would help him create greater work.

After completing his studies at the university, he moved to Tokyo and worked with the *Stars and Stripes Pacific Bureau*. They publish an American military newspaper that focuses on and reports on matters concerning the members of the United States Armed Forces. As a team member, he brought photos to the newsroom to be reviewed.

He learned to always ask, "What is the story, what is this photo saying?" The eyes of the team would appraise the images and identify the stories if they were being told in the photos. Images with no story were ripped up and thrown away.

The newspaper experience provided another opportunity to learn from mentors. As he listened and observed, he gathered information about the workings of a newsroom. He developed a greater understanding of the importance of how news photography provides a narrative of the event.

A photograph is a powerful tool for storytelling. It chronicles a heartwarming event, or it reveals a horrible injustice that incites rage. Some photographs had such a strong message that repercussions were felt across America and the world. For example, a snapshot of homeless children in a warzone eating from a trash can ignited outrage. Or a village scene with an innocent injured mother with a child caught in the conflict of war kindled loud antiwar narratives.

His career continued with a volunteer assignment to Iraq. With a combat camera in hand, he was transferred. On this assignment, he began to shoot with video. Some good stories were canned others were published. Although his combat camera saw little hostility and even less action, he pleasingly stated, "Iraq was a good gig."

He enjoyed Iraq, yet he was ready to capture new adventures on film. He requested and received orders for an assignment on board a ship in South America.

Completing his Southern Hemisphere duties, he then transferred to Italy. This new, and exciting location provided fresh opportunities to tell stories with his work. Here, just like all the other assignments, his skills increased. Expanding his craft, he developed the ability to edit and package photography for publicity and promotion.

While in *Stivale (the boot),* he had a life-changing event. In the country of romance, the adventuring artist made a more personal request that was granted. He proposed to and married the love of his life in the land of Saint Valentine.

After marriage, he began to plan for civilian life. His work transitioned from photojournalism to a more polished commercialism style.

No longer in the service, he continued to evolve as an artist. While actively creating art, he perfected his craft with additional studies in art and design. He became a graduate of the Art Center College of Design in Pasadena, California.

No doubt, he was born to create art, and with the support of mentors, great education, and a vast amount of experience, Stolz's work demonstrates tremendous growth. Through the journey, his photography took a personal turn. Today, the artistic work has a fine art aspect. He describes his work as, "John Candy meets Hemmingway, and they have a baby."

Currently, living in Los Angeles, he is a freelance photographer. He specializes in editorial, lifestyle, and portrait photography. He is skilled in studio and 'on location' shoots. Working closely with clients, he produces visually appealing content from start to finish, including coordinating shoots, scouting locations, defining shot lists, set lighting, producing imagery, and editing post-production.

Over time, the photographer developed the philosophy that you must have fun with your craft. He confessed; he continues to "push" himself to have fun. He proclaimed, "If you are having fun, everything you create will be better."

This story began with a time in his military career when he 'pushed' himself out of a helicopter. "Pushing oneself" is a lesson the successful artist learned early in his life when mentors played a powerful role.

He acknowledged the role models of his youth imparted life skills, along with lessons on how to live life successfully. Early in his life, he wisely learned to benefit from sagacious mentors.

Kenny Hooker, a scout leader was the first mentor to "push" him out of his comfort zone. Chris said, "He dared me to know my own skills and worth." With that lesson, the young scout began to live his purpose. The valuable mentorship taught him a lot about how to live life. He learned the flow and importance of networking. He was taught the value of teamwork.

Chris vividly recalls learning how to work as a team through a team-building exercise the mentor taught. The leader filled an ammo box with supplies and hid it in the woods. The assignment for the boys was, as a team, to find the supplies. The objective was to survive. The goal was to develop teamwork. This is one of the many times he remembers learning a valuable lesson.

Most importantly, he stressed, "The scout leader knew that a moody kid would eventually grow up and need self-reliance." Then, with sincerity, he continued, "I appreciate those lessons more every day." Chris and his first mentor have remained connected through the years.

He appreciates other mentors in his life as well. One is Debbie Diamont, a former TV reporter and retired local teacher, and the other is Brack Llewellyn, founder of the NoneSuch Playmakers, a local stage director, playwright, and actor. Chris is thankful for all the influencers in his life. They taught him to have fun with his craft; he daily reminds himself of that lesson. He believes his mentors fueled his mediocrity in creating art and "pushed" him to be more artistic. (see Appendix III Beyond MAin...Live Theatre and Performers)

The Mount Airy Photography Club brought him back to town to give a lecture on photography. The local photography club is hosted by the Surry Arts Council and led by local photographer, and Chris' mentor Kenny Hooker. Chris said he was happy to come back home and share his art and experiences.

I met the artist, after he gave the presentation at the Earl Theatre, in downtown Mount Airy. The presentation was outstanding, the art was MAmazing, and the man was inspiring. I was awed by his sincere appreciation for his mentors who taught him to "push" through adversity and become self-reliant.

I wrote this story from the notes I took during his lecture, communication with the artist, some printed articles, websites, and my own opinions about the power of the "push" to influence our direction.

Everyone needs a role model who can influence their life. The influencer can teach you how to "push" yourself to success. Without the "push", we often remain in mediocrity.

In one period during the history of ancient Israel, they had lost drive and self-reliance, but the prophet inspired them to turn toward success, he proclaimed hope until the captives 'pushed' themselves to being self-reliant.

Today, you can mentor and "push" or you can allow yourself to be influenced by being "pushed", whichever, be great.

Our small town has many heroes who have been pushed to greatness by caring mentors.

www.christopherstolz.com

Photographer Christopher Stolz

Resilience...Linda Shubert

It had been two years since Linda became the innkeeper of the charming historic home, but as if it were yesterday, she remembered what her son had said soon after guests started arriving.

"We have the world come to us; we meet so many people." He said in amazement. Linda often thinks about his words, especially when she recalls so many people coming from so many different places.

The out-of-towners come from all fifty states, and they come from all walks of life. Reflecting on their diversity, she said, "Everyone who visits with us becomes our friend and they feel like family." Then, pinching herself, with questioning awe, she whispered, "Are we living in this beautiful house?"

Elbert and Linda Shubert meticulously restored the 1886 Queen Anne Victorian and created a gorgeous bed and breakfast filled with southern charm. The house is nestled two blocks from downtown Mount Airy. It has five guest rooms, all artistically arranged.

Steps from the home is a garden patio on top of a hidden fallout shelter installed by the original owner Eugene Smith, the brother of Katharine Smith Reynolds who was born in Mount Airy and became the wife to the tobacco tycoon R.J. Reynolds.

Their love of art led the Shuberts to name the renovated inn The Vermeer Bed and Breakfast and Art Gallery, deriving its name from a Dutch innkeeper, and artist Johannes Vermeer. It is one of several B and Bs in and around Mount Airy. (see Appendix III Beyond Main...B and Bs and more lodging)

Linda is a culinary artist and Elbert is a plein air and portrait artist. Her artistry is seen daily in the cozy dining room. His artistic creations, along with other artists' works can be found throughout the inn.

Elbert's studio is located on the first floor, and often you find him there working on various projects. Throughout the year, he hosts classes and workshops.

Whether you are an artist or a fan of the arts, you will enjoy the art and pottery displayed throughout the inn. If you enjoy painting plein air, you are invited to bring your easel and paints. North Carolina, and especially the foothills provide beautiful vistas waiting to be captured on canvas.

Although beautiful, this story is not about historic houses, canvas creations, or intriguing guests. This vignette is about resilience.

Bouncing back in the face of adversity requires resilience. Linda, a strong woman, attributes her ability to rebound to her independent spirit, which she learned from her dad.

Sometimes, to the extreme, he taught the family independence. For example, she remembers growing up in the country, far away from stores. Only bordering farms were nearby. When they were out of sugar, her dad's independent spirit forbade them from borrowing a cup from their neighbor. He would drive one hour to the nearest store to make the purchase.

In adulthood, she discovered life has more challenges than an hour's drive for a cup of sugar, but the independence she learned as a child would help her survive. Although she is acquainted with health crises, family losses, and personal tragedies, she does not think the difficulties in her life have been as severe as others.

Through it all, she survived and learned to thrive. Each mountain of adversity taught her new coping skills and helped her to develop inner strength

Many people are born with an undeveloped ability to bounce back from adversity. Some never bounce back while others do. Some have discovered with each new trial they can learn new ways to overcome.

Linda is one of those persons with the ability to bounce back. She learned to grasp faith, take steps to go through difficult times and she learned to be a victor, not a victim.

She thinks, even though you feel you are alone and without help, there is always a bit of strength waiting to be grasped. You can pull your boots up and march on.

Marching from the farm, and becoming an adult, Linda followed her dreams for happiness. She married and began to build a family. She began a nursing career and her husband worked in sales. They grew their family and soon there were two darling daughters.

There were normal day-to-day struggles that any newly married couple faced. When the family moved from North Carolina to Florida, they would face life-changing challenges.

They had been in the Sunshine State for just a few weeks when tragedy struck. Her husband was working while Linda, with friends, took the little ones to a lake house to celebrate the 4th of July.

Filled with laughter, the small kids played in the cove, while the grownups waited patiently, taking turns skiing. It was Linda's turn. With the excitement of a thrilled child doing something for the first time, she jumped into the refreshing warm water.

Immediately, excruciating pain pierced her leg. Drifting like a dead limb, her leg floated to the top of the water. With fearful wide eyes, she gazed at her dangling limb while becoming painfully nauseous. The knot on her knee looked as big as a watermelon.

In a furry, her friend scooped her up while calling for help. He told another friend to watch the girls. Like a NASCAR driver, they raced 20 miles to the nearest hospital in a Podunk town.

As the X-rays were being taken, to no avail, they tried again and again to reach her husband.

Gazing at the two-dimensional screen, the emergency

room nurse saw the top of the knee was shattered. "Oh my god, Oh my god!" She yelled with an alarming shriek. The freak accident had torn the skier's ACL and MCL.

After reviewing the options, and being unable to walk, the patient requested to be taken to Jacksonville Orthopedic Institute. She knew the Jaguars Sports Specialist, who worked there, and trusted him to do the needed work.

It took three days before the hardware for surgery arrived. After days in the hospital, the three-month process of healing continued at home.

At home, things grew more difficult. Her hospital bed had to be placed on the lower level of the house. The girls needed attention and were afraid because mom could not walk. Her husband became angry because she could not work. The bills piled up. The water was cut off. Dealing with the healthcare system increased the stress, it was exhausting.

Eventually, things began to settle, and she was able to do some paperwork from home. Mustering extra effort to take care of the household and working while confined to the bed, she climbed out of the pit.

After overcoming the accident, more darkness crept into her life. Her husband developed a serious drug addiction. The self-destructive behavior led to family alienation. There were extreme highs and devastating lows.

Now there were three girls, each of them experiencing the pain of a drug-addicted dad. One Christmas, the family reached a breaking point.

She went to the grocery store with the three little ones in tow. After gathering the staples and attempting to checkout, something happened, it felt like time stopped. There was a problem. The manager was called, and Linda was given the news.

Insufficient funds. There was no money in the bank account. Nothing left for food, much less Christmas gifts for the girls. The drug-using dad had been slowly draining the account, day by day, $20 here, $50 there. He had drained the whole account.

The stressful situation grew worse. After years of coping, one-night Linda was awakened by her drug-addicted husband. He said, "I'm not ready to be a dad, I plan to leave the marriage." Without notice, he abandoned them.

She found herself a single mom, away from her family. Isolation kicked in but independent strength took over. Financial and personal struggles grew. Things worsened when he fled the area to avoid child support.

Now, the maverick mother solely supported the family, and finances were stretched. The strength of her inner woman said, "That which doesn't kill me will make me stronger."

Through grit, determination, and her independent spirit, the self-supporting mom developed the ability to be resilient. She said, "I can make it." She struggled and climbed to become a director of nursing in a 200-bed facility.

Barely getting by, things continued to be difficult. The lone breadwinner took control of her future direction and furthered her education. The goal was to get a better job with more pay.

It was during that time that she met Elbert. Her self-reliance breathed relief as she learned how supportive a gentle, kind, loyal, and hardworking man could be.

It was a time of crisis for them both. He too had been disappointed in a relationship. They connected with mutual support and common chemistry. They completed each other and encouraged each other in faith.

She describes their marriage and blended family as bliss and more bliss, filled with blessings. In future challenges, the independent woman had a helpmate. And he found a woman that invigorated his talents.

His artistic dreams were birthed in his youth. As a teenager, his ability to sketch demonstrated his talent. For most of his adult life, he wanted to be a full-time artist. Few people cheered him on to pursue his passion. Some even discouraged him. Eventually, he stopped drawing.

His new wife with the 'can do' spirit did not want him to go through life always wondering "what if". She wanted him to shine. She wanted him to pursue a career as an artist. She encouraged him to draw, sketch and paint. Challenged by her resilience, he began a self-portrait. He said, "What will you say if it is bad?" With a heartening expression, she smiled.

The finished work was amazing. "It was fabulous!" She boasted.

Together, the couple has overcome great obstacles and accomplished great things in pursuit of their dreams.

With roots in North Carolina, the happy Shuberts visited their family for Christmas five years ago. While there, they remembered this cute little town called Mount Airy. With a few extra days to visit, they decided to explore. Off they went.

They found the people to be so friendly. They recall people stopping on the street and asking, "Can we help you honey" The experience made Elbert smile. He said, "I can live here." As fast as a flash, they both fell in love with the small-town atmosphere.

They made plans to move to North Carolina. They began to investigate various locations. Wanting to live in an 'artsy' community they looked at the western part of the state but were drawn to Mount Airy. In a short time, they contracted to buy the house on Taylor Street. It just felt like home.

Feeling at home she said, "There are many favorite things I love about Mount Airy. Most important is the sense of community." She further elaborated by saying, "I have been accepted here even though I am an outsider."

They experienced the normal adjustment period moving from a city of five million to a town of 10,000 but the Shuberts know they have found home. Every day, you can find them sitting on their porch, listening to the birds, and appreciating the fauna. "Even in winter you see the Blue Ridge Parkway, it never gets old." She spoke with satisfaction. "We will never live in a big town again; we plan to stay here when we retire."

Their dreams were fulfilled.

The Shuberts have one more dream before they retire. They envision a local thriving art community. Currently, a few artists live in the area. They hope more will move here as more locals discover their artistic gifts.

The arts have always been a part of Mount Airy, and with the inspiration of an artist like Elbert, our art community will grow. Currently, the local arts community is flourishing with murals, street art, art shows, studios, artistic programs, newly discovered local artists, and an Arts and Entertainment District downtown. (see Appendix II More on MAin...Art Scene)

Today, it looks like the Shuberts are flourishing. Through it all, Linda has cemented her belief that you can be an overcomer.

She said a lot of things I went through bolstered my confidence. "I survived." She affirmed, "I look at the glass half full, not empty, with each new challenge, I remember, I have been through difficult times before, I will get through this."

Through determination, she did not complain or give up. She said, "There are so many stories of struggles, some people have pity parties while others inspire you. The best thing about being a nurse is that God connects me to countless people with inspiring stories."

She shared one of those stories. Although her friend, Mark Silverstone has passed, she continues to be inspired by him. In his 20s, he had a paralyzing diving accident which he says saved his life. Confessing, he said I was on the wrong path.

Although confined to a breath-controlled electric wheelchair, he could shrug his shoulders and move his hand and fingers slightly. With a specialized computer, he earned a master's degree, wrote poetry books, and worked as a counselor. Paralyzed, he was independent. He never complained. She affirmed. "I know so many inspiring people like him."

"You need to find joy wherever you are, you have to bloom where you are planted." She spoke in wisdom. Addressing difficult situations in life she continued, "It is what it is, focus on the positive, negativity will make you a bitter person. You will miss blessings if you are bitter about the past."

Her "can do" resilience matches the "can do" spirit that prevails in our small town.

The restored home has become a private residence and the Shubert family moved to Pilot Mountain to start their next adventure. Elbert continues to paint and Linda continues to enjoy life in North Carolina.

Sugar...Darren Lewis

One of the sweetest memories I have is watching my grandmother, Esther Reynolds, carefully remove the blackberry deep dish dessert from the oven and place it on the counter to cool. I remember the crystal particles sparkling on the perfectly baked lattice-topped crust. I can smell the fruity aroma filling the air. The warmth of those sugary memories lives on.

With ample sugar, this familiar dessert is called a sonker, it is easy to make, and its uniqueness can only be found locally. (see Appendix III Beyond MAin...Sonker and Sonker Festival)

Over the centuries assorted types of sugar have derived from various sources with varying names. George M. Rolph, in his book *Something About Sugar*, states that the original source of sugar from sugarcane predates the eighth century BC and originated in India. The Subcontinent calls it jaggery. This may very well be the beginning of the sweet and popular part of today's human diet.

The Pew Research Center using USDA data discovered that Americans eat 77 pounds of sugar each year. That is a lot of sugar. And I bear witness, as a southerner, that we may consume more sugar than the average American.

We do love our sugar in more ways than one. Even our country colloquialism takes advantage of the word to convey a variety of meanings.

Most every southern small-town conversationalist knows how to use the word sugar to communicate much more than something sweet to taste. For example, it is common to use the word as a term for old-fashioned endearment, politely seasoning our speech with adulation. When addressing those we love, we often call them sugar.

On the other hand, the jargon could express veiled criticism. Calling someone sugar can cloak the conversation with an opportunity to disparage someone we may have less affection for. A true southerner easily discerns the difference, while others may have more difficulty interrupting the true message.

The sensitivity of society paired with our desire to be genteel provides another opportunity to disguise our feelings. The creative selection of softer words with hidden meanings communicates our real messaging with less offense.

Sugar is one of those words that can veil our feelings. Many people strategically say 'sugar' when they might be tempted to swear. The substitution requires control, forethought, and the spirit of sweetness.

Darren Lewis, a local from Pipers Gap, grew up being influenced by our local gentility. From his youth, he is familiar with the different meanings of our 'sweet' conversations. (see Appendix III Beyond MAin...Gaps)

Darren Lewis

for a game on the Pickleball Court. He is a good athlete and a skilled player. I was impressed by his placement of the ball and paddle technique. He is disciplined and a strategic player. (see Appendix III Beyond MAin...Pickleball Courts)

During our competitive game, a fault was made. With control and conviction, he firmly said "Oh sugar." Yes, sugar!

A wide smile covered my face, as I reflected on the double meaning unique to our dialect. I chuckled. Not only was he strategic in his game, but he was equally deliberate and measured in his choice of words. Admiring his seasoned thoughtfulness, I wanted to better acquaint myself with this giant of a man with a gentle spirit.

I scheduled an interview with him. Relaxed, sitting in his office at the Reeves Community Center, he opened his heart. I discovered his journey. Like many, he knew the pain of loss, yet his life path was filled with an optimistic caring spirit.

Often, it is grandparents that fill our lives with a caring spirit. Their loving influence has a lifelong effect on our lives. Their memories warmly guide our journey.

Darren's positive influences would come from other sources. Three of his grandparents died before he was born. The only grandparent he knew passed when he was an adolescent. Unfortunately, these were not the only losses the young man would feel. At the age of 17, his mom died. He watched as she bravely fought a battle with cancer. Few young men his age experience that journey, and fewer know the inner brokenness, fear, or anger that can arise when a loss is experienced. He said this was the most challenging thing that ever happened to him.

When your world is turned upside down, you often feel alone, and you must learn to navigate through the unknowns. For many facing this type of challenge, it becomes easy to develop resentfulness and channel anger in non-productive ways but not him. He was the youngest of eight children, and the only child still at home when the family experienced loss. Naturally, with added responsibility, and the isolation of the loss of a mom, he developed leadership abilities. His natural and growing strength enabled him to pilot through the next difficult journey. After the death of his mom, his dad's illnesses grew worse. For the next five years, he was there for his dad as he trudged through dialysis.

In his early 20s, Darren would not only know the loss of all his grandparents, and his mom but now his dad. He was one of a small number of young men who knew the loss of all parental figures.

He would not remain alone. He said one of the greatest things that ever happened to him was meeting Rebecca, his wife, and building a family with her three sons.

The second greatest thing that happened to him is his professional career. It started part-time in high school. During his summer breaks, he worked at the local community recreation center. During his college days, a full-time position opened for him. He was hired as the Athletics Supervisor.

As a young man, he developed sensitivity to underprivileged kids he worked with at the center. From his early days in recreation, he worked with youth, especially reaching out to deprived youth. His passion fed his life's calling to be a professional in recreation focusing on disadvantaged youth.

For more than 30 years, he has been a part of the recreational landscape. He served as Director of the Mount

Airy Parks and Recreation Department before being assistant city manager. Throughout his career, he has been a successful leader. He is personally responsible for the department receiving the Innovative Program Award in 2006 and he continues to bring innovative programs to the department.

Sometimes, the losses we experience provide fewer advantages, privileges, and opportunities for success in life. It becomes easy to blame our lack of success on disappointing events in our life, but like Darren, despite adverse situations, we can overcome and learn to be successful and fulfilled in life. Through all the disappointments and losses in life, he seized the opportunity to help others with fewer advantages, and he developed the skills to reach out and lift them.

Life may not always be a fairytale but life sure can turn out to be sweet. You can turn disappointments into something better. Darren had no control over life's disappointments, but he had control over his reactions.

Early, he learned that words matter. Words can change and support a positive direction.

A constructive spirit sprinkled with sweet words gives us the strength to carry on. Words come from our hearts and have a powerful influence over our situation. Words create and can change our environment. Our words support our inner beliefs with affirmations. The potential power of words can change your environment.

We can learn from the southern use of the word sugar. When you are tempted to use a swear word you can strategically replace it with sugar. By reframing, we better manage adverse situations.

You have the choice; you can season your life with a little more sugar. The words you speak are powerful, they can sweeten your day. Mary Poppins sang everything is better with a spoon full of sugar.

With intention and directional strategy, you can change

your life.

Our small town is filled with people who reframed their sour situation and turned it into sweetness.

Grandma's Peach Sonker - some call it The Lazy Sonker
- 1 stick of butter, put in a deep dish (8" x 8") and place in oven to melt
- Beat these 3 ingredients together to form the batter 1 cup self-rising flour, 3/4 cup sugar, ¾ cup of milk
- Prepare 2 – 4 cups of fruit – ¼ cup of sugar, stir and pour in bottom of the dish
- Pour batter evenly over the fruit, drizzle with melted butter
- Sprinkle lightly with sugar (or cinnamon)
- Bake at 350 degrees for 30 minutes or until done (brown on top)
- Optional add 1 tsp of baking powder, and 1 tsp of vanilla extract to batter
- Ingredients, time, and temp vary based on the size of the dish and amount of fruit

One of many local sonker recipes – most families have one.

Survive...Edith Thomas

The word "boom" describes a lot of things about the decade of the 1950s. The economy, housing, and the birth of babies were growing in record numbers. The swelling affluence created a sense that the all-American family was financially secure.

The Golden Age of Television gave the impression that everyone was living in prosperity and bliss. Even the popular shows with single TV dads, from *Little Margie to Bonanza,* portrayed flourishing families. It would be another decade, before the beloved *Andy Griffith Show* would air, starring a single dad with a more modest but comfortable lifestyle.

It would take longer, two decades, before a TV sitcom depicted the life of a single mom, *One Day at a Time.* The 1970s TV show highlighted the struggles that a single mom faced, but nothing on the TV sitcom came close to the real-life struggles of Edith Thomas.

She was a woman, raising a family in the 50s, who lived through harsh struggles. She learned how to survive in difficult times. Her ability, to overcome challenges, gave her strength to not only survive, but she learned how to thrive.

She was born in Dry Pond, Virginia in 1930. Dry Pond is about 15 miles northeast of Mount Airy, just across the Virginia state line.

One-month-old Edith faced her first critical challenge as a motherless infant, her mom died a few weeks after she was born. Her father needed to work, and the infant girl needed a mom, so arrangements were made, and her aunt, who lived several miles away, took the baby to her home to nurture.

At the age of three, her dad remarried. He and the stepmom wanted to bring the child home. The little girl recalls being carried on horseback through the woods, on a muddy road back to her home of birth. She remained in Dry Pond until she was a young woman. At the age of 18, she moved to Mount Airy to work and married one year later.

At that time, the effects of WWII were ongoing. Some goods continued to be rationed into the mid-fifties. Many families had no spare money, and without modern luxuries, housework was more difficult and most married women did not work outside of the home.

The exploding prosperity after the war, visualized in the sitcoms, would not be felt by many families until later in the decade. For Edith, the financially good times would come even much later.

Financially, her first husband did not contribute to the family's needs. She said he was a dreamer. He seldom held a job for long, and when sporadic wages were made, he often squandered the money. The mom became the only stable wage earner for her growing family, soon to be a household filled with seven children.

Edith Thomas

It was difficult being a woman, a mother, the sole provider, and the manager of the modern-day conveniences. She worked from sunup till midnight to provide for her family. She hand-washed everything. All the children's clothes were sewn and mended by hand. Independently, she made sure the children had food on the table.

Each day started early, feeding the kids, and getting them ready for school, then she was off to the textile mill for a day's labor, then home to feed the kids, wash and mend the clothes, take care of the upkeep of the household, make sure noses were wiped, scrapes were bandaged, and the children were loved and nurtured. Burning the midnight oil, many nights she crawled into bed exhausted.

Money barely met the needs, but necessities were met and most of the time, bills were paid. Without any type of social services, the breadwinner developed the skill to survive. Through skillful ingenuity, she learned to generate income. She seldom ever missed work and to make more money she began to do alterations on the side for others. It was beneficial that she did not mind hard work and to her advantage that she loved sewing.

Once she rented out the top part of the house to keep housing for the children. She and the seven kids moved into the basement to live.

During one of many difficult times, the income streams would not pay all the bills, she was about to lose the home, and the seven small children would be homeless. Up until that time, she had never asked anyone for help, she carried the burden to sustain the family by herself. But this was the worst challenge she had ever faced. She went to her sister for relief. Her sister gave her enough money to keep the house. She proudly gushed, "I paid every penny back to her."

Another time, the opportunity to open a community store helped bring additional income into the home but it led to long hours. After finishing an eight-hour or more textile job, she worked in the store and ended each day by sewing.

Her talent in needlework developed by constantly sewing for the children and her skill as a gifted seamstress was refined by tailoring garments for neighbors, friends, and even strangers. Someone was always asking her to mend, alter or sew something and she always said yes. She became an expert seamstress which helped increase income to sustain the family of seven children, a working mom, and a deadbeat dad.

People in the community do not know her for living a difficult life, they know her for helping other people. One of her daughters, speaking with great respect recalled, "I saw how she always put other people first, often doing without so someone else could have." Even during the most trying times of her life when she needed help, she continued to help others.

Her sister vouched for her generosity, "There is a special place in heaven for Edith, because of all the kindness she has shown to others. They broke the mold when they made her." No one in need is ever turned away. Whether it is groceries or money, she shares whatever she has.

She not only gave in a time in her life when she struggled, but she continues to help now that days are brighter. Recently, a lady came to her and asked for money for transportation, and without question, Edith provided it. She explained, "I did not expect her to pay me back, I gave because there was a need."

Looking back, her children have great admiration for her dedication, and they idolize her survival skills. One daughter said she sacrificed every day. Her youngest child said, "She taught me how to survive, she taught me how to scrape and get by and she taught me how to sacrifice and reach my goal of going to nursing school." Today, her daughter, the nurse is the CEO of the local Hospice.

Her other children have also learned and benefited from Edith's strength. Two own businesses, one a salon, and one owns Mayberry Primitives (an embroidery and gift business at 215 North Main Street). The other children have successful lives. Each of them overcame challenges in life, completed careers, and built their own family and home. (see Appendix II More on MAin...Businesses Downtown)

Her personal history is an amazing story of overcoming. Like the hazards of climbing a rocky mountain, throughout her life, she was acquainted with constant struggle and difficult situations, but she mastered survival. The arduous times she lived through taught her that you can make it through tough times. Tough times make some people hard and bitter, but not Edith, her struggle made her extra kind and more generous. She identifies with people who struggle.

In her 80s, she began working part-time at the *Fabric Menagerie*, at 111 North Main Street. It is a fabric and sewing business. It has been open and thriving, for more than 45 years. The store provided the perfect place for her adept expertise.

Her lifelong love of fabric, sewing, tailoring, and making alterations, made it her dream job. She became remarkably close to the owner, Paula Eubanks.

When Paula became too ill to manage the store, Edith began operating the business. Because of her big heart and love for the fabric business, she first took over without pay. She did not want the shop to close.

For about a year, she managed the store, sold fabric, and supplies while keeping up with alteration requests, then she made an offer to buy the inventory and rent the building. In May 2019, her offer was accepted.

Today, the 90-year-old survivor is living her passion. The business (her home away from home) is housed in an unpretentious building across the street from the Jack Loftis Plaza and on the corner of Main and Pine Street by a small city park called Lowry Park. (see Appendix II More on MAin...Jack Loftis Plaza and Lowry Park)

In Lowry Park are two metal art pieces. One is entitled David. It depicts the shepherd boy and his stories of struggle and survival. He did not have kingly weapons, but he faced giants with confidence and faith, and he always overcame them. He learned you never give up. (see Appendix III Beyond MAin...Metal Artist and City Parks)

Just like David, and the stories of strong men and

women across the globe, the story of Edith is about struggle and survival. Everyone faces giants. Since her struggles as a motherless child, she acquired the ability to overcome them. With an overcoming spirit, she survived bigger giants in life as the sole provider with seven children.

Survivors, like her, demonstrate that determination, hard work, integrity, honesty, faith, and persistence reward success.

Survival has taught her many things. She has learned to treasure truth and honesty. Even in trying times, she said you can keep your word. With experience, she spoke wisdom, "If you can't keep a promise, let them know, just be honest."

She learned you could take control in difficult times, and you can overcome. She wisely voiced "Do what you have to do, there is another day coming, if you live, it will get better. Look around, you will always see someone in greater need than you are."

She is so inspiring, I often drop by the fabric shop, just to say hello. One afternoon, I asked, "How do people learn to survive?" She said, "First you have to pray, then pull yourself up and do what is necessary to get back on your feet. Just don't give up."

Edith is one of many who have lit the path, showing us how to survive.

In our small town, accomplished people survive because they never give up.

Tragedy...Ramon Milian

Teary-eyed with passion, the brawny Puerto Rican spoke with conviction, "Tragedy teaches you so much more than success."

I did not expect such emotion while having lunch at The Loaded Goat. What I knew was soon affirmed, 'In real life, tragedies cannot be averted'. (see Appendix II More on MAin...The Loaded Goat)

In 1978, Ramon Milian was born in Puerto Rico but has called Mt. Airy home since 2007. He is a professional employee in the local Carport Industry (see Appendix III Beyond MAin...Carport Industry). His mom, wife, and three children have fallen in love with the advantages of living in our charming small town. The Milians are active in the community, faithful in faith, and perfect examples of the success of the all-American family. But sometimes tragedy precedes success.

A son of an alcoholic dad, he had a problematic life growing up in Puerto Rico. He is the youngest of four siblings and the only boy. Often alone, he learned to be self-sufficient. Each morning he would cook and iron his clothes before walking to school.

Although things were difficult as a child, he was taught the values of Puerto Rican culture by his grandmother. She taught that "Familismo", or family is the foundation for social structure. The concept is based on the Spanish system of "compadrazco" or co-parenting which includes grandparents as part of the immediate family. The tradition places the grandmother in a revered position as a great influencer who teaches the family principles.

His grandmother taught him manners and etiquette. She taught him to never lie to a female but respect her. To this day, he never walks in front of a lady except to push the button for her in an elevator. He was taught to be hard-working and positive. Although his early life was harsh, the guidance from his grandmother established a solid foundation that in the future enabled him to rise above despair.

Youthful disappointments caused him to grow angry and bitter during his teenage years. His mom, also unhappy and discontent, moved to Washington state looking for a better life. The troubled young man soon followed.

While stateside, he became the prodigal son. He made life decisions that led him on a destructive path. He allowed family connections to be broken. Life became even more difficult. He experienced the tragedy of homelessness.

Thinking the challenges in Puerto Rico might be better than homelessness, he went back to his boyhood home on the Island. Once again, he was living with his dad. Little did he know that greater tragedy was ahead.

Before the "horrendous tragedy" that was a defining moment in his life, he met Azalea, his true love. Amid love, tragedy continued lurking, cloaked under fleeting happiness.

In 2003, the happy couple was driving to a New Year's Eve party. The mood was expectant and festive. Life was good.

Their happy life changed in a moment. Without warning, from nowhere, a metallic death machine on four wheels came hurtling into their peaceful path.

To avoid the impact, he stomped the brakes with intense force. With a swift glance at his lover and a faster plea to God, he tried to manage the moment. Hoping to avoid the crash, he jerked the wheel piloting the car as it skidded 300 feet. Losing control, he recklessly swerved only to make impact.

Boom! The sound like thunder pierced his bones. A lady nearby saw the frightful faces of those in the colliding cars. The couple was tossed like limp puppets.

His injuries were severe. His spinal cord was bruised. Due to the extreme swelling, permanent damage was probable. His back would tingle for months. The forceful impact of the wreck popped his capillaries. His shoulder was damaged requiring more than 70 therapeutic treatments to heal.

However, the mutilation to his body was not his primary concern. During and after the horrific crash, he could only think of his pregnant lover. In the moment of spinning out of control, he shouted, "God take care of my family!"

After spiraling and colliding, it felt like time stood still. The moment felt like an eternity. Again, his thoughts raced toward Azalea. In a flash, he gazed at her. Hastily processing the damage and accessing her apparent lack of injuries, he focused on the unborn. There were no visible signs of injury. Not realizing, nor considering the degree of his injuries, he scurried to her side. Promises, prayers, and petitions were all gushing in hope of making a deal with Deity.

The faint sound of sirens intensified. Lights were flaring. Medics were diligent. Soon they were racing to the trauma center, the ambulance rushed off with the flower of his life. As the sound of the first siren was fading, he was being prepped for transport.

All the way to the hospital, he continued to desperately beg and bargain, "God save my family." Promises of a changed life were made. After arriving at the hospital, it took more time than he had the patience for, but soon the news came. Azalea was unharmed, but the baby did not make it.

Time stopped again. The room became icy. He felt that none of his prayers had been heard. Examining his past, he reasoned that nothing good had worked out in his life. He angrily questioned. "Where is the love the church talks about? Hurting, he began to wrestle with deep bitterness.

After the accident, fury, and agony became daily companions. During the next few months, the strength and love of his companion aided in lessening the pain. The *familismo* joined in to help with the healing. His, previously absent, dad stepped up to support him. In the process, they became great friends.

The inward pain, which had been swelling for years, was shrinking. Tormenting questions began to find answers. But transformation was born with a phone call.

Two months after the tragedy, the woman who had seen the accident and their faces as they collided called to see how they were doing.

He shared the progress of how he and his Azalea were healing. Then she asked how the other man in their car was doing. She said, "I saw him reach from the back seat and put his arms around your wife to protect her while you were wrecking."

Ramon was silent. A moment felt like an eternity.

His thoughts spun in his head. There had been no one else in the car. In that instant, he realized God is love. With thankfulness and grace, he gratefully proclaimed, "Azalea, the love of my life is safe."

After the transforming call, and acceptance that God is love, he began to write a new life chapter called "the lessons of tragedy".

The couple in love grew spiritually and nourished their family. In less than a year, Azalea was pregnant again. With love, they continued to triumph in all areas of their lives.

The big heart, his mother said he was born with, began to surface. With watering eyes, he remembered his tragedies and with sober-mindedness, he said, "I don't deserve my wife, but she has stuck with me."

He permitted his pain to properly prioritize his life. First, is love. Love of God, love of wife, love of children, love of family, and love of community. Next, he learned to trade tragedy and pain for living. He learned that life is precious. Each day he cuddles his daughters, kisses his wife, and gives his son loving advice.

Truly, tragedy had been the teacher that led to success. Love is success. He said, "I am no longer a life filled with tragedy, but I am living a life filled with love and success."

While he was happily building a family in Puerto Rico, a happier transition was brewing. Some friends had told his mother about a nice small town called Mount Airy. She visited and discovered its charm. Soon, she moved to make it her home.

Valuing family, Ramon felt it was important to be near his mom as she aged. Soon, they moved to be near his mother and the Milians became part of our small-town family.

For many years, they have called Mount Airy home. They are role models in our community. The Puerto Rican culture coupled with love fits perfectly with our small-town values.

They teach their children that your word should be your bond. They teach their kids to be humble and honest. Recently, they were asked to present their family mission statement to the school board. Together, they shared the key to their success: "Let love be the driving force."

Truly, a lesson can be learned from tragedy.

Our small town has many people who have overcome tragedy, some were born here, and others were drawn here.

Ramon and Azalea Milian

Wisdom…Tony Martin

I discovered my dad was a wise man. The older I grew, the wiser he became.

The more I aged, the more I learned my life is filled with wise people.

Over the years, my admiration for wisdom continued to grow. Today, I revere wisdom. I long to sit at her feet to acquire a greater understanding of the important things in life. I think wisdom sets a meaningful direction. It leads to destiny. Destiny brings fulfillment.

The discovery and development of the local granite quarry provide an example of how wisdom builds success.

The usefulness of the largest open-faced granite quarry in the world was not always known. In the 1880s, Thomas Woodroffe, a rail line developer understood the value of the 90-acre exposed rock and made a wise purchase. The fruit of his wisdom provided a feast for success and gave Mount Airy its first nickname, the Granite City. (see Appendix III Beyond MAin…The Granite Quarry)

Historically, many of our residents have demonstrated wisdom, allowing our little town to develop, evolve, and grow even obtaining international fame. Examples of wisdom are seen in the historical transitions that have sustained us.

From the birth of a village, from the pioneer "hollows", a town grew. The natural trail that ran through our town supported its growth.

It was aided in development by the wise advertising of our area as a healthy 19th century mountain retreat with healing sulfur springs. Many tourists were drawn here to the resort. When the White Sulfur Springs Resort fizzled, farmers with insight grew our economy with agricultural and tobacco commerce. (see Appendix III Beyond

MAin...Hollows and White Sulfur Springs)

As farming diminished, innovative businessmen established textiles that prospered our families until the financial benefits of textiles seeped to other countries.

In decline, innovative entrepreneurs grew several national carport corporations, at the same time small business owners wisely identified our town as Mayberry, once again bringing tourists to town.

Added to the growing tourism, agriculturists with insight promoted our county as an emerging "wine country" and was federally designated as an American Vinicultural area. Currently, there are 21 wineries in our county. (see Appendix I Things to do in Mount Airy...Wineries)

Throughout our history, local wisdom has allowed the town to overcome and reinvent itself after each major economic shift.

Today, the actions of clever people continue to help sustain us, often utilizing the model of small-town American charm to ignite present-day economic development. Again, we are on the cusp of progress.

Each day, on Main Street you pass people full of insight and imagination who are wisely applying their knowledge to situations and thereby enhancing society with success. However, far too often, the voice of wisdom is unheard because we do not take the time to listen. The wise ones among us are like rare jewels that need discovery.

In my opinion, Anthony (Tony) Martin is a local gem not to be missed. He is a cultured world traveler, skilled pilot, and successful entrepreneur. He is a dynamic person who like so many others was attracted to the charm of a friendly and active small downtown.

Tony's refined life, his urbane wife, Yuana, a former flight attendant, and their delightful family enhance our diverse community.

One New Year's Eve, I sat at a table near the Martins for a sumptuous feast at the Old North State Winery. World-renowned chef Chris Wishart prepared a crafted menu. (see Appendix II More on MAin...Old North State Winery and Fish Hippie Company)

After our dinner at the Winery, we went across the street to the Regional Museum of History. The museum hosted the annual midnight Sherriff Badge Raising (in keeping with the Mayberry theme). (see Appendix II More on MAin...Mount Airy Regional Museum of History)

I found myself laughing, talking, and celebrating the New Year Eve's event with the Martins. As the celebration was winding down, everyone was making plans to leave. Just like ole friends, I was asked to continue the festivities at their home on Cherry Street, only a couple of blocks off Main Street.

I remember as a young man riding through Cherry Street. I would admire the architectural designs and the beautifully manicured yards. Those memories made me more excited about the exquisite home I was about to visit.

After arriving, immediately, I felt comfortable in the chic setting. Following an hour or so of laughter and conversation, I began to admire the art on the walls.

Tony invited me to the study to see another work of art. As I walked into the study, I was immediately drawn to the penetrating eyes of T. E. Lawrence (a painting of the original Lawrence of Arabia). I was invited to sit.

My host began to share some of his escapades, along with insights. I took note of the remarkable acumen acquired through his experiences.

Knowledge and insight flowed like gentle streams. Early in the conversation, He asked, "Have you ever read *Seven Pillars of Wisdom?* Hungry for more information, hoping he would continue sharing, I slid to the edge of my seat and replied with a thirsty tone "No." He continued to share.

As I continued to marvel at the portrait, he enriched my mind with the historical life of T.E. Lawrence, occasionally, sprinkling the narrative with his exploits.

He enlightened my dim understanding of the man in the framed, life-sized painting that had captivated my attention along with his personal stories.

Elucidating the story of World War I, he reasoned that many of our current Middle Eastern problems would be minimized if different decisions had been made during that time. He proceeded to share how that Lawrence's insightful advice would have changed the course of history had the world powers followed his wisdom.

No doubt, Tony is a sagacious man, who knew what he was talking about. During tragic times, he had made wise life-changing decisions.

His unique life experiences as a navy man and a private pilot for some of the most well-known people in the world provided him the opportunity to walk in wisdom. A nondisclosure agreement prevents him from naming the long and impressive list of private passengers. Some requesting his service were high-end politicians, celebrities, former presidents, and some of the wealthiest people in America.

His rich background, formal education, life experiences, and spirituality have all played a role in the wise man he has become. Added to that, he is an all-around nice guy that enriches the lives of those in association with him.

Tony's family is from Ararat, Virginia, about 10 miles from downtown. But his fondest memories are working with his dad in the hardware store he ran, located on Main Street. Growing up, he spent a lot of time on Main Street.

Recalling, the hotdogs and breaded hamburgers at Snappy Lunch, haircuts from our famous barbershop, and assembling Western Flyer bikes, he warmly shared his memories.

After a successful aviation career, those fond memories, coupled with a professional change, caused Tony to return to downtown.

Narrowly escaping death through a horrendous

motorcycle accident that devasted his life, he journeyed through a dark season. He said, "Losing the career I loved, I had a pity party, I felt my identity was gone."

After a couple of years, he began to see there were other things to live for. With a fleshly frame, a half-metal body, and applied wisdom, he refocused, "It is not about what I have lost, but it is about what I still have, and I'm still here."

Speaking about the trying time in his life, he revealed. "I didn't feel like I had much wisdom, but I decided to pull myself out." Tony clearly stated he had other things to live for. Redirecting his destiny, he decided to call Mount Airy home.

Our downtown is enriched by the Martin family. In my opinion, their association with the local wine industry, along with their insight of the expanding wine-making trade in our area, led him to a wise purchase.

He bought *Un' Corked*, a business located at 126 Main Street in historic downtown. He turned it over to his wife to run. Yauna, his beautiful wife, and a modern successful business-woman oversees the day-to-day operations.

It is a premiere wine shop with a wine bar that specializes in local Yadkin Valley wines. They offer a curated selection of over 100 local wines, California wines, boutique wines, and craft beers from around the country.

Yauna Branner Martin

Being cognizant of the area's budding wine trade and taking advantage of an acquisition opportunity demonstrates astute business expertise. Wisdom is in the timing. Wise and timely decisions birth success.

Like Lawrence of Arabia, like area leaders, and like Tony, you will make destiny decisions during critical times in your life. These judgments determine your future successes.

It is important to exercise prudence in your journey as you make life-altering decisions. Your future and your destiny are elevated by those choices.

You have important decisions to make. Think about it, meditate on the opportunities in your life, ask for wisdom, and allow clarity. Wisdom will unlock your success.

Mount Airy's many successes are the result of wise people in our small town.

Proverbs 16:16 Wisdom is better than gold, and insight is better than silver.

Conclusion

Thanks for visiting Main Street.

I hope you found the spirit that makes Mount Airy a great place to live and visit. The inspiring folks you met may help you understand why I think the small-town idyllic community is not a myth.

I believe the wholesome spirit found here can be anywhere. Even in the inner city, with complex problems, I know calm neighborhoods where people care and connect.

Before the birth of a metropolis, families built communities with neighbors. Our nation's landscape is sprinkled with little towns and communities that depict our national ideals.

The diversity in our small town is often overlooked, but I tried to capture its distinction by representing the whole community of people who built the spirit of small-town America, aka "Mayberry".

Mayberry fans have identified more than 150 citations, used from Mount Airy and weaved into The Andy Griffith Show. People, names, businesses, streets, objects, and many locations from Mount Airy and North Carolina can be seen throughout the 249 episodes filmed in eight seasons, from 1960 to 1968. While reading the book, I hope you found many of them.

With purpose, I sprinkled each story with ample things to do in Mount Airy. The interesting details and amazing facts enable you to experience our small town.

The Appendices provides the most inclusive list of opportunities and offers a great resource for any traveler.

I desire that you have discovered why many people love the idea of small-town America, aka Mayberry. I hope you have enjoyed your visit. Please come again and again to my hometown, the best small town in America.

Appendix I

Things to Do in and around Mount Airy
This is not an exhaustive list, there are more things to do, especially in the county and region.
Visit the Mount Airy Visitors Center for more information, 200 N Main Street, Mount Airy, NC 336-786-6116 www.visitmayberry.com

Tours
Downtown Ghost Tours
Squad Car Tours
Trolley Tours
Mayberry Spirits Distillery Tours
Winery Tours (21) One on Main
Gertrude Smith House
Backstage Tours Andy Griffith Playhouse
Visitor Center Guided Tours
Walking Tours/Bike Tours

Museums
Regional Museum of History
Andy Griffith Museum
Eng & Chang Exhibit
Earl Theatre
Aunt Bee's Exhibit
Thelma Lou Exhibit

Historic Homes
Andy Griffith Home (Hampton Inn rents)
Gertrude Smith House (seasonal)
Edwards Franklin House (seasonal)
Moore House Tour by appt.
Tucker Home Tour by appt.

Trails
Paddling Trails
Cycling Trails
Hiking & Biking Trails
Tour Fishing Trails
YadkinValleyNC.com/map
www.elkinvalleytrails.org

Entertainment
Arts/Entertainment District (seasonal) food trucks, artists, and live music
Merry-Go-Round 2nd Oldest live radio show
Blackmon Theater Summer Concert Series
Street Jams Thursday/Saturday
Earl Theatre (free Thurs. night) plus $ shows/movies
Andy Griffith Playhouse
Creekside Cinema
Live Music downtown restaurants (weekly)
Winery/Vineyard Performances (weekends)
Nonesuch Players – Seasonal Community Theatre

Golf
Cross Creek Country Club
White Pines Country Club
Hardy's Custom Golf (nine-hole Par 3 & miniature)

Arts & Monuments

Whittling Wall
Veteran's Memorial
Women of Bluegrass
Art Walk & Sculptures
Art Studios
EG Shubert Gallery
The Studio
Valkyrie Gallery
Vincent's Legacy Rocks
Groovy Gallery
Street Art (Market St.)
Murals
Fiddle Crawl
Metal Sculpture Garden
Lilly P & Mally S Studio/Gallery
Talley's Custom Frame and Gallery
LazerEdge Wood Art

Mayberry Sites

Snappy Lunch
Otis' Jail
Sheriff's Office
Darlin's Cabin
Betty Lynn Display
Aunt Bee's Room
Walker's Pharmacy
Floyd's Barber Shop
Barney Impersonator Home
Andy's Home
Wally's Service Station

Historic

Easter Brothers Music Store
Andy Griffith Home
Granite Quarry
Historic Rockford & Candy Store

Festivals

Farm Fest (May)
Mayberry Cool Cars & Rods Cruise Ins Monthly
4th July Celebration and Parade
Ukulele Retreat
Girls' Night Out (Spring/Fall)
Mayberry Days (September)

Sports & Activity

Greenway 8+ miles walking/biking
Kayaking & Canoeing
Disc Golf
Golf
Pickleball
Fishing
Horseback Riding
Putt Putt
Bowling
Skating
3 Par Golf
Batting Cage
Sports clubs/gyms

Family Adventure

The Corn Crib
The Farm
Miss Angel's Farm
White Sulfur Springs
Pilot Mountain State Park
Cousin Emma's Tea
Carolina Ziplines
Scoops Metal Sculpture Garden
Bike Rental

Campgrounds

Veteran's Park
Beechnut Family
Mayberry
Byrd's Branch
Mom & Pops
Jomeokee
Greystone

Craft Breweries

White Elephant
Thirsty Souls
Uncorked (wines/craft beers)
Midsummer Brewing, Westfield
Angry Troll Brewing, Elkin
Skull Camp, Elkin

Sonker Festival (October)
Autumn Leaves Festival (October)
Budbreak Wine/Craft Beer Fest (August)
Food Truck Fest (Spring/Fall)
Ole Time Fiddler's Convention (June)
Blackmon Amphitheatre Summer Series (April – September)
Mayberry Farmer's Market (May – October)
Moonshiners and Racers Reunion (September)
Mayberry Truck Show (October)
Student Film Festival

Distillery
Mayberry Distillery

Farm Recreation & Services
Homeplace
Borrowed Land Farm
Minglewood Farm & Nature Preserve
Miss Angel Farm
Our Chosen Heritage Farm
Ridenour Ranch
The Farm in Dobson
Dock Southern Farms

Wineries
Adagio Vineyards
Carolina Heritage Vineyard & Winery
Elkin Creek Vineyard & Winery
Golden Road Vineyards
Grassy Creek Vineyard and Winery
Haze Grey Vineyards
Herrera Vineyards
Hidden Vineyard
JOLO Winery and Vineyards
Jones Von Drehle Vineyards and Winery
McRitchie Winery and Ciderworks
Old North State Winery
Pilot Mountain Vineyards and Winery
Rayson Winery and Vineyards
Round Peak Vineyards
Serre Vineyards
Shelton Vineyards
Slightly Askew Winery
Stoney Knoll Vineyards
Surry Cellars

Wedding/Event Venues
Absolutely Country Wedding Barn & Event
The Depot at Cody Creek
Coley Hall at The Liberty
Cross Creek Country Club
Elkin Creek Vineyard
JOLO Winery & Vineyards
Klondike Cabins at Grassy Creek Vineyard
Luna's Trail Farm & Event Center
Mayberry Meadows
Mitchell River House
Moore's Spring Manor
Rosa Lee Manor
Round Peak Vineyard
Serre Vineyard
Shelton Vineyard
The Barn at Blueberry Hill
The Barn at Heritage Farm
The Barn at Windfall Farm
The Farmhouse Siloam
Valley Brook Farm
White Sulfur Springs

Appendix II

More on MAin

Art Scene...Several local artists honored our musical heritage by dotting the sidewalks in the heart of the city with 20 painted sculptures within a three-block area. The artwork is seen in the form of painted guitars, banjos, and fiddles. Each piece of art tells a local story. Added to them, ten metal sculptures, by Chazz Elstone, are placed in the downtown area for public viewing.

Several murals adorn downtown buildings with more planned. (see Melva's Alley and More Murals).

A team of local artists painted decorative displays on the cement manhole covers along the Greenway, surrounding the town. The art highlights local scenes, mountains, and landmarks. In the river that runs by the Greenway, primitive artist, Raymond Goehrig has stacked rocks creating vertical works of art for people to enjoy.

The recent development of the Market Street Arts and Entertainment District downtown is growing the art community and increasing art events. Seasonally, on weekends local artists gather and display their work.

Throughout the year, our local library and the local Arts Council host art displays and sponsor art classes.

A true landmark in the community is the 40-year-old Talley's Custom Frame & Gallery located in the heart of downtown. It is one of the few remaining shops left in the area to offer the art of framing. They have shadow boxing, matting, molding, picture glassing, and custom framing, along with a variety of prints for sale.

Area galleries are expanding. Currently, EG Shubert

Studio is in the Vermeer Bed and Breakfast. The Studio with Lilly P. & Mally S. visual artists and Valkyrie Gallery is at 140 North Main Street. Vincent's Legacy, creator of the Kindness "Rocks" is located there. Periodically, an Artist's Market is held at the same location.

Award-winning street art can be viewed on Market Street, our Arts and Entertainment District. Local high school students painted multicultural art on the parking spaces and the walkways.

The Groovy Gallery opened in 2021. It is a joyful makers' space, gallery, and vintage boutique. They offer art classes. Located at 527 West Lebanon Street.

Bakeries and Candy Stores...Two bakeries are near downtown: Pastelicious, only 1.3 miles from downtown at 906 West Pine Street; Mill Creek General Store, only ½ mile from downtown at 541 West Pine Street. Bakeries downtown are the following: Sweets by Sarah, 237 North Main Street; Anchored Sweet Treats and Savory Eats, 139 Moore Avenue and Miss Angels Heavenly Pies, 153 North Main Street.

Two Coffee Houses downtown offer baked goods, Pages Books and Coffee - 192 (#200) North Main Street and Keep Smiling A 'Latte - 162 West Pine Street.

Candy Stores downtown are the following: Prudence McCabe Confections, 192 (#400) North Main Street; Bear Creek Gifts and Candy Kitchen, 165 North Main Street; and Opie's Candy Store, 135 North Main Street.

Businesses Downtown...There are 92 businesses and shops downtown Mount Airy including 11 Salons and/or Barbers. In addition, there are realtors, lawyers, accountants, financial planners, plumbers, insurance agents, nonprofits, galleries, and a computer repair shop. New businesses continue to open in our growing downtown.

Fish Hippie Company...FISH HIPPIE has captured inspiration from life on or by the water and provides premier original styles each season. The operation is locally owned and in 16 states and more than 230 retail locations. In 2020, the Mount Airy outdoor lifestyle apparel brand added light manufacturing of medical supplies including PPE and masks. A small retail space is located on Main Street in the Old North State Winery, a larger store is located just north of town. 336-415-5165

Festivals...Mayberry Food Truck Fest; Downtown Art Walks; Public Art Guitar Crawl; Budbreak Wine & Craft Beer Festival; Mayberry Farm Fest; Mayberry Cool Cars & Rods Cruise In Events are monthly; July 4th Parade and Celebration; Mayberry Days Festival; Autumn Leaves Festival; Girls Night Out Events; Moonshine & Racer's Reunion; Veteran's Day Parade and Program and Downtown Christmas Parade. There are other fun and exciting downtown events throughout the year. Not only downtown, but year-round numerous events and festivals are held in Surry County at venues, farms, and wineries.

Granite Churches on Main...For one mile and a half stretch, there are six granite churches on Main Street. Beginning on South Main (across from Wally's Service Station) there is Mount Airy Friends Meeting, going north for two blocks is the First Presbyterian Church, and continuing north for about eight blocks you come to the oldest, which is Trinity Episcopal. Continuing north, on the right is Frist Baptist, the largest granite church. Proceeding north next is Holy Angels Roman Catholic, and then Grace Moravian, Andy Griffith's home church. The history of these churches can be found in the Regional History Museum or on the Trolley Tour. There are other granite churches in town as well as granite houses. See www.surrydigitalheritage.org for more information.

Groovy Goose and Thrift Shopping...The vintage store is located one block off Main Street, on Market Street, which is an active area with block parties, fairs, craft breweries, shops, a yoga studio, and a gaming and hobby store. The store focuses on items from the 1960s and 1970s, though the owner boasts she has groovy things from all decades. It is a fun shop with an enormous inventory. Downtown, within walking distance, there is more thrift store shopping.

Is Mount Airy, Mayberry?...When you visit Mount Airy, you can step back to a simpler time. It is no coincidence that a stroll down friendly Main Street reminds people of the town of Mayberry. You can visit Floyd's Barber Shop, Walker's Soda Shop, and Snappy Lunch. Replicas of the show are seen at Wally's Service Station. Researchers of the show have found more than 150 references from streets, and businesses, to people from Mount Airy and surrounding areas. In episodes, you can see many things from Mount Airy, including the Mount Airy News Paper, and hear discussions about the Bear Mascot for the local high school. On top of the Blue Ridge Mountains, only seven miles from where Andy's mom was born, is a community called Mayberry. As a boy, Andy visited there many times. The small-town ideals portrayed on the show are lived every day in our small town, Mount Airy, North Carolina.

Jack Loftis Plaza...The Plaza is a result of Jack's community service and includes a plaque in the former Mayor's likeness, public restrooms, tables, chairs, and a directory wall map of downtown. The area is heavily used. It is especially busy during festivals and weekly outdoor musical jams. It is a great place for visitors downtown to take a break from shopping and enjoy a snack while resting. A mural of the famous gospel group, the Easter Brothers, is in the plaza. 112 North Main Street

The Loaded Goat...The Loaded Goad is Mount Airy's veteran-owned, family-friendly sports pub and grill. Jimmy, their mascot, and their name are inspired by an episode of The Andy Griffith Show. In Season 3; Episode 18, Cy Hudgins comes to town with Jimmy, his goat. He is told that he could not have Jimmy in the barbershop. Cy ties him up outside. Unfortunately for everyone, he gets loose and makes his way to a construction shack used by a road crew and eats a crate full of dynamite. The rest of the show is about how Andy, Barney, Otis, and others interact with Jimmy to get him safely out of town. The restaurant's burgers were voted the best burgers in North Carolina. 247 City Hall Street. 336-755-3627

There are 23 restaurants in the downtown area within a 1 ¼ mile stretch.

Lowry Park ...Located on the corner of Pine (a Blue Star Memorial Highway) and Main, the aesthetic tiny park has a Historic Earl Theatre informational marker, three benches, beautiful flowers, a Leave a Book/Take a Book Library Box, and two sculptures in steel created by Chazz Elstone.

Elstone is a local artist and owner of Scoops Ice Cream (located in the Pine Ridge Area). The four-foot metal art creations are entitled David's Jubilation and The Psalmist. Eight other pieces of his metal art are displayed outside, around the downtown area.

The park is named to honor the Lowry family, who voted in our first local election. One member of the family served as a longtime commissioner. Jennie Lowry, the owner of the Ole Mill Music Store on Main Street, is a descendant. Her great-great-grandfather provided a printing service to the City and served as the first editor of the first newspaper in Mount Airy. Only two blocks from her business, he had a printing store and owned an organ manufacturing company. One of the organs he made is on display in the Regional Museum of History.

Melva's Alley and other Murals...Melva's Alley is a pedestrian area off Market Street by the Thirsty Souls Community Brewing. The Alley has lighting, tables, chairs, flowers, a plaque, and a mural of the international famed blues, jazz, and gospel singer. Although, originally from Memphis, she chose to live in Mount Airy. On the opposite side of the building where Melva's mural is painted on Thirsty Souls' building, there is a Beer Mugs small mural.

Coca-Cola has a two-story mural first commissioned by the Coca-Cola Company in 1915. It was restored to its original state by Coke and located in the alley at 185 North Main Street.

Franklin Street Flower Mural by local artist Madeline Matanick is located on Franklin Street, by a downtown parking lot.

Barn Quilt Murals are located on Moore Avenue between Main and Renfro Streets and more on Market/Oak Street.

Easter Brothers Mural, famous gospel singers from Mount Airy, is in Jack Loftis Plaza on Main Street.

Hey from Mayberry Mural is at the Andy Griffith Playhouse.

More murals near downtown can be seen at Mill Creek, both outside and inside. And on a building on the corner of Pine/Independence.

Mount Airy Downtown, INC offers a grant program to commission artists to do new murals or public art projects. An Andy Griffith Mural and a Donna Fargo Mural are planned.

Miss Angel's Heavenly Pies...The baking is done the old-fashioned way, from scratch, no preservatives, using the finest ingredients, with fresh fruits and berries from their 65-acre farm and orchard. Anyone passing by cannot resist the heavenly smells from the daily freshly baked goods served by a friendly staff. There are over 28 pie flavors including custom pies and cakes. They even have the signature Mountain Moonshine Pie made with moonshine from our local Mayberry Distillery. They have all types of other pies, muffins, cannoli, tiramisu, breads, pie art, gourmet cookies, Sonker (Mount Airy's one-of-a-kind dessert), pot pies, quiche, and other lunch items.

People from all over the country visit her store each year. She has gotten statewide and national publicity through TV shows, news reports, newspapers, and magazines.

Mount Airy Museum of Regional History...The Museum is home to over 35,000 square feet of permanent exhibit space over four floors. Exhibits cover nearly every topic imaginable. You can see what life was like for Native Americans and early settlers in "the hollows." Experience an authentic turn-of-the-century country store, learn the history behind the largest open-face granite quarry in the world, and listen to the Old-Time music that is unique to this region. While at the Museum you discover our many "hometown heroes"; Donna Fargo, Tommy Jarrell, Andy Griffith, and Chang and Eng Bunker (the original Siamese twins). Exhibits change often and include traveling exhibits on loan. 301 North Main, 336-766-4478

Mount Airy Visitors Center...A must-stop for every visitor. The Visitors Center is a hub of activity, located in a large granite building on the corner of North Main and Moore Avenue. It was the First National Bank, built in 1893, originally a brick building and refaced with granite c. 1912. The bank printed $776,600 worth of national currency and stopped printing money in 1935.

The Visitors Center provides information on local events, tourist sites, restaurants, or lodging. Step-on-guides are offered with prior arrangements. They are open 7 days a week and provide complete information on the following: Mount Airy, and touring sites; restaurants, and lodging; Surry County, and historical sites; Yadkin Valley Wine Region, and vineyards. They have staff to go over a map with you and tell you about everything to see and do in the area. 336-786-6116

When in the heart Lf downtown, look for the Clock, located on the corner of Moore and Main, and you are there.

Old North State Winery...Housed in a former Hardware store built in 1890 on Main Street. Ben and his wife Ellie have successfully created a fun, hip, upbeat atmosphere combining wine-tasting tours, a cool ambiance, outstanding food, live entertainment, and events to create a true experience. Daily dining is available for lunch and dinner featuring locally grown and freshly prepared specials by world-renowned chef Chris Wishart.

The winery still has the original pressed tin ceiling and solid oak floors. It is open with tasting tours available. 308 North Main Street 336-789-9463

Replicas of the Andy Griffith Show...Wally's Service Station was a real service station that opened in 1937 and closed in 1986. Andy Griffith knew him. Located on the block where the service station is located, there are replicas of the show: Emmett's Fix-it Shop, Mayberry Hotel, The Darlin's Cabin, Mayberry Court House, The Sheriff's Office, and Otis's Jail Cell. 625 South Main Street, only six blocks from downtown. On Main is Floyd's and Walker's Fountain.

Aunt Bee's Room, a collection of Aunt Bee memorabilia is located at the Mayberry Motor Inn. 501 North Andy Griffith Parkway

Floyd's Barber Shop is located downtown beside Snappy Lunch. Both were real businesses, that Andy visited.

Restaurants Downtown...Starting on Main Street at the corner of Independence you will find the following restaurants:

Kyoto Japanese Restaurant is located one block off Main Street on Independence.

Going south on Main, one-way, from Independence Street, on the right is Leon's, home of the California Burger. They also have home cooking.

Continuing one block south, to Oak Street, you can go left one block to The Loaded Goat, (voted the best hamburger in NC), and right one block to Market Street where you have Thirsty Souls Craft Brewery which offers artisan pizza and other specialties.

Pass Oak Street, staying on Main Street, you have two restaurants on the right. Mi Casa, fresh Tex Mex, and Sweets by Sarah with specialty sandwiches and sweets. On the left, you have Barney's Café with sandwiches, home cooking, and daily specials.

At the Moore Street light, turn left and ½ way down the block on the left you will find Anchored, Sweet Treats & Savory Eats with quiche, sandwiches, and more. On the right is State of Graze with Charcuterie Boards and one-of-a-kind salads/sandwiches.

Continuing south one block on Main Street, go to the Franklin Street light. Just to the left, you have Paige's Coffee Shop with pastries, turn right on Franklin Street and you have two more restaurants.

Soho Bar & Grill will be on the right and Kazoku will be on your left, about ½ block down Franklin Street. Soho has a Vietnamese flair, with sushi, tacos, burgers, and more, while Kazoku features steaks and sushi.

Back on Main Street, as you go through the light at Franklin Street, just to the right you have Mayberry Home Cooking and Walker's with burgers and sandwiches.

Continuing south on Main, walk past Walker's Soda Fountain, on the right you have Miss Angel's with quiches, pot pies, and more, then you have Snappy Lunch with sandwiches and the famous Pork Chop Sandwich.

Turn right off Main Street at Pine Street and you have one coffee shop and a bakery (Keep Smiling A 'Latte)

Going north out of town on the parallel Rockford Street you have McDonald's and a little further north to Lebanon Street you have Gondola Italian Restaurant.

Going south on Rockford, for about one mile, you have Subway, Chase & Charlie's By the River, Speedy Chef, and the Derby Restaurant.

There are approximately 23 restaurants in the downtown area within 1 ¼ miles.

Stock Car Racing Wall of Fame…Mount Airy Stock Car Racing features all the original greats who helped stock car racing become a major sport. Stock car racing is said to have originated during the U.S. Prohibition period (1919-

33) when moonshiners needed faster cars to evade the law. Cars were modified to make them faster. Drivers, sponsors, flagmen, mechanics, moonshiners, photographers, historians, and more are honored with plaques and pictures on the wall. Located in a small alley across the street from the Historic Earl Theatre.

Tours...A variety of tours are available, following is a list:

Trolley Tours –picks up at hotels and Main Street. It is available for private parties, weddings, birthdays, or special events. www.mayberrytrolleytours.com

Squad Car Tours – starts at Wally's and covers downtown, the quarry, and Andy highlights. 336-789-6743

1939 Cadillac Fleetwood Imperial Limo Tours – operated by Heart and Soul B & B, and takes you to wineries, or a night on the town. You must be a guest at the B&B to reserve the tour.

Walking Ghost Tours – start at the Regional History Museum and begins at dusk. 336-766-4478

Mayberry Spirits Tours – offers an entertaining experience giving the history of moonshining and the current process of making whiskey, or barrel bottling with tasting, plus gourmet extracts, and cigars are available. www.mayberryspirits.com 461 N South Street

The **21 wineries** located in our county each offer vineyard, and/or distillery tours. www.yadkinvalley nc.com/guides/surry-county-wine-trail/

Frog Holler Wine Tours – transports to different wineries. www.froghollerwinetours.com

Seasonal Tours – local farms and historic homes offer seasonal tours. Gertrude Smith House (closes during the winter), Moore House, Edward-Franklin House, Horne Creek Living Farm, Tucker Home, The Farm, The Corn Crib, and garden clubs provide garden and Christmas tours. Ask the Visitors Center for additional farm or home tours.

Visitor Center Tours – Step-on guides available by appointment. 200 N Main Street. 336-786-6116

www.visitmaybery.com

Walking/biking tours or private car tours – contact **Calvin Vaughn** at 336-749-0816 or lifeonmain@ yahoo.com

Tribute Artists…A full cast of tribute artists visits Mount Airy during the year, especially Mayberry Days. https://www.themayberryeffect.com/cast Even Andy Griffith's daughter and her friend fill the role of "The Fun Girls" during Mayberry Days. Their enthusiastic appearances help bring Mayberry to life. Brett Harris, a local tribute artist lives on the same street Andy lived. Non-Mayberry characters include Larry Isenhour who performs as Elvis and Roger Lineberry performs as Michael Jackson (moved to England)

Wally's Service Station…Once a service station and was mentioned on the Andy Griffith Show. Today it is a gift shop and where the Mayberry Squad Car Tours begin. Nearby are replicas of the show. Emmett's Fix It Shop, Mayberry Motel, Darlin's Cabin, Otis's Jail, and Mayberry Courthouse. Located six blocks from downtown. 625 S Main Street.

Whittling Wall…The artful wall pays respect to local people who have helped shape our history and culture. It depicts artisans, musicians, educators, small business owners, and hard-working people who represent the diverse character of our town. The following persons are featured on the wall: The Whittler represents the local history of citizens, who gathered at the wall; Tommy Jarrell, a legendary fiddle player; Fred Cockerham, a renowned banjo player; Ralph Epperson, founder of WPAQ Radio Station; Donna Fargo, a famous country singer, and songwriter; L.H. Jones, a groundbreaking public educator for the African American Community; Floyd E. "Flip" Rees, a businessman who led the way in downtown revitalization; and The Mill Worker, representing the thousands of women and men who worked in local textile mills.

Brad Spencer, a North Carolina artist, created the brick

sculptures. The intent of the project is to spark thought. It is the hope of our small town that you see yourself in the people represented on the wall, and that you ask yourself the question: "How can I make my community a better place for future generations?"

Appendix III

Beyond MAin

African American History:
   JJ Jones School...In 1914, JJ Jones, an African American educator (and his wife) were hired to teach at the Virginia Street Elementary School. In 1935, his son Leonidas became the principal of the first and only African American high school, called the Mount Airy Colored High School. Later it was renamed JJ Jones School. The school taught the students trades, and the students helped build the gym and auditorium. Through the inspiration of the gifted teachers, many of the graduates became successful business owners and leaders in the community.
   Rosenwald School...Thousands of schools were built primarily for the African American population in the early 20th century through a fund created by Julius Rosenwald. The philanthropist was a clothier who became part-owner and president of Sears, Roebuck, and Company.
   Satterfield House...Located at the corner of West Virginia Street and North Franklin Road. Built in the 1890s, it was one of the first African-American-owned properties in Surry County. On the four-acre site, there was the Rosenwald campus. There is a current focus on preservation.
   Tucker Home...Charlie and Ollie Tucker, a rural black couple in the farming community of Pine Ridge, both were children of slaves. They married and worked hard to save their money to purchase 10 acres of land for $70 and built a home in 1914. Charlie worked in the coal mines of West Virginia, and Ollie boarded teachers, grew fruit and

vegetables to sell, repaired shoes, and ran a cider mill. They continued to buy small parcels of land and soon acquired 85 acres along Tucker Road, where three generations of Tuckers have continued to live. The home is restored to museum quality.

Freetown...A community about three miles south of Dobson where many free African Americans lived.

More African American history can be seen in the Regional Museum of History on Main Street.

Andy Griffith...(June 1, 1926 – July 3, 2012) He was an American actor, comedian, television producer, southern gospel singer, and writer whose career spanned seven decades in music and television. Born in Mount Airy, North Carolina, he had a modest home life. His first interest in theatre began with an elementary talent show. In his teen years, he continued performing in school, community theatre, and churches. He attended UNC Chapel Hill University, first to study to be a minister, but changed his major to music after getting involved with campus theatre. He began teaching during the week and performing on weekends. His first national success came as a monologist performing, *What It Was, Was Football*. Nominated for a Tony, he had success on Broadway. In the 1950s, he debuted in movies. He went on to act in more than 28 films. His sitcom success began in 1960. He won a Grammy for a gospel album. He was married three times and adopted two children with his first wife. He is buried on his estate in Manteo, North Carolina.

Andy Griffith Homeplace...Guests can rent and stay in the home where Andy Griffith lived. The house contains antiques and is decorated in the 1930s-1940s style with Griffith memorabilia. The boyhood home is within walking distance from downtown Mount Airy, and many tourist sites. Reservations are made through the Mount Airy Hampton Inn. Amenities include cable, maid service, continental breakfast at Hampton Inn, and use of their facilities. 336-789-5999

Bed and Breakfast...There are four B & Bs in or near downtown: Heart & Soul B & B is in the historic district downtown; Bee's B & B is three blocks from Main Street; The Vermeer B & B has an Art Gallery and five guest rooms; and Cousin Emma's B & B is a pre-Civil War historic home on South Main Street.

Surry County has three B & Bs: The Rockford Inn B & B is in the historic town of Rockford; it is an 1848 Antebellum farmhouse; located on the eastern slope of Pilot Mountain is Pilot Knob Inn B & B; and Singleton Lodge & Cabins is a seven-bedroom inn with private cabins.

Additional area lodging includes a dozen hotels/motels, along with area cabins. The Visitors Center provides lodging information. 336-786-6116

City Parks...Mount Airy has nine parks: Lowry Park, Main/Oak Park, Graham Park, Tharrington Park, H. B. Rowe Environmental Park, Riverside Park, Veteran's Park, and Westwood Park

Carport Industry...Leonard's, a 50-year-old company, is one of the oldest metal building companies in the area. Today, there are more than 32. Some of the top metal building-producing companies in the country are based here, generating multi-millions of dollars in sales each year. Several are owned by Hispanic members of our community who trace their beginnings to family members who were migrant workers in the agricultural field and learned the metal building business. A true American dream and immigrant success story. If you include builders, call centers, customer service, design, sales, contractors, and corporate office employees, the industry may be the largest employer in our area.

Community Large Musical Groups:

Golden Notes…is directed by Sylvia Lowry, she and her husband traveled with Donna Fargo and lived in Nashville as performing musical artists before moving back to their hometown. The choral group she directs practices at the Surry Arts Council and performs for free in the community. The choir sings gospel, older music, and patriotic songs.

Maui…is directed by George Smith and is a large ukulele group that practices and performs locally. The Surry Arts Council hosts an annual Ukulele Retreat.

Voce…is a choral ensemble that provides outstanding concerts.

Mountain Valley Voices…is a talented hospice choir that has a CD, Sounds of Home. The large choir is talented and performs by request.

Communities and Towns in Surry County:

The County is filled with things to do, from ziplining, unique dining, farms to visit, fun festivals, and 21 wineries.

Towns in our county are the following: Dobson, our county seat; Pilot Mountain, or Mount Pilot on the Andy Griffith Show; Rockford, a historic area; Toast, more like a community; and Elkin, with a population of 4100.

There are numerous communities: some are nearby in Virginia. Cana, VA, five minutes on HWY 52 (North); Fancy Gap, VA, top of the mountain, fifteen minutes on HWY 52 (North); Ararat, VA, fifteen minutes on HWY 104 (Northeast). Several communities are in our county: Flat Rock and Slate Mountain (Northeast); Bannertown and Ararat, (South); Sheltontown, Westfield, and Holy Springs (Southeast); White Plains and Zephyr (Southwest); Pine Ridge, Red Brush, Beulah, and Lowgap (West). There is an Ararat, NC (South).

The naming of each community has local folklore revealing its origin. For example, locals say that Red Brush was named for the dry, red clay dust that settled on the bushes along the side of the road, giving them the 'reddish' color.

The Visitors Center provides information on area events/activities. 336-786-6116

Dairy Center...Located at 407 W. Lebanon St., opened in 1954. The restaurant seats less than 30 people but has curbside service. It was originally known as the Chicken in the Rough. Then it was a Dairy Queen for a few years before it became the local landmark, the Dairy Center. They are known for their hotdogs, ground steak sandwiches, and homemade ice cream. They have won awards and they have been featured in magazines.

Donna Fargo…Our local hometown girl's first platinum album, The Happiest Girl in the Whole U.S.A., established her as an award-winning singer, songwriter, and performer. With her second single called Funny Face, Donna became the first woman in country music history to have back-to-back million-selling singles. She received numerous awards and starred in her syndicated variety show, The Donna Fargo Show. Mount Airy honors her with a statue, museum display, and naming a highway after her. Her home was a few miles east of town. She lives in Nashville writing books and cards. www.donnafargo.com

Gaps…Gaps, or passes, are breaks or low spots along mountain ranges or ridges. If it is very narrow, it is called a gorge. Gap is mainly used in the southeastern United States. The gap is used for transportation or communication into or away from areas. Some gaps in our area that lead into the Blue Ridge Mountains are Willis Gap, Pipers Gap, Fancy Gap, Low Gap, Volunteer Gap, and Wards Gap. All of them go to Virginia. Virginia is a few miles north of Mount Airy.

Granite Quarry…It is the world's largest open-faced granite quarry in the world. On the surface alone, the quarry encompasses about 90 acres or roughly the equivalent of 66 football fields. The mass — the block you cannot see — is about 7 miles long and 1 mile wide, north, and south. It is 8,000 feet deep. It has been mined since 1889 and has enough rock to last another 500 years. Mount Airy granite is widely recognized — including such high-profile projects as the World War II Memorial in Washington, D.C.; the Arlington Memorial Bridge; and, here in North Carolina, the Wright Brothers Memorial — but it is also popular for curbing, especially in Northern states. Granite Quarry Trail, Mount Airy www.ncgranite.com

Greenway…The Granite City Greenway System comprises more than 7 miles and is being expanded. The Greenway borders Lovills Creek running along HWY 52 and the Ararat River, which runs along Riverside Drive. The Greenway circles the city, and features several pedestrian, parking, and canoe/kayak areas of access. It is the location of several City-sponsored events, as well as 5k, 10k, and ½ marathons. A dog park is on the Lovills Creek side and Riverside Park is on the Ararat River side. People walk, run, bike, picnic, play in the water, canoe/kayak, and fish along the greenway. See the Visitor's Center for more information on Bike Rentals. https://www.mountairy.org   /349/Parks-the-Granite-City-Greenway

Historic Radio Stations:

WPAQ…started in 1948, it airs the second oldest radio show in America (after the Grand Ole Opry). The Merry-Go-Round features live performances from the historic Earl Theatre every Saturday. The station features Old Time Music, Bluegrass, and Gospel. 740 AM and 106.7 FM and reaches worldwide audiences online. Since the 1950s, its sister station, WSYD airs from the same building.

WSYD…airs a mix of pop oldies from the 50s to the 80s, as well as beach music. 1300 AM and 105.1 FM, and reaches worldwide audiences online.

Hollows…Peter Jefferson (Thomas Jefferson's dad) surveyed the area in 1747 and found three families living in the hollows. As early as the 1750s settlers began to gather in the area now known as Mount Airy. It became a stopover point on a much-traveled road that ran from Salem (now Winston-Salem) into Galax, Virginia. Moravian records identified the area as the "hollows."

Ice Cream Shops…You can enjoy ice cream in most restaurants in Mount Airy, but there are several specialty ice cream shops. Downtown: Whit's Frozen Custard, Hillbilly Gluten Free Bake Shop and Creamery, Opie's Candy/Ice Cream, and Walker's Soda Fountain. Around

Mount Airy or in the County: Scoops Ice Cream and Such, Aunt Bea's, CF Jones, Speedy Chef soft serve, and the Dairy Center.

Jam Sessions...Downtown each Thursday night at the Earl Theatre is a FREE Jam Session. Other Jam sessions occur downtown on the street, frequently on Thursday evening or Saturday morning. Bluegrass and Old Time Music Jams are held nightly somewhere around the county. email randy@mtairychamber.org for jam locations/times. During the annual Fiddler's Convention, jams break out all over town.

Jimmy Lowry...A Mount Airy musician. Locally, he played with The King Bees, and later The O'Kaysions ("I'm a Girl Watcher") and several other regional groups. He and his family moved to Nashville to be one of five Mount Airy musicians, which included John Rees, Russell Easter Jr., Steve Jarrell, and Larry Miller who played for Donna Fargo. He went on to serve as Donna's band leader for more than a decade. He later joined Steve Jarrell & the Sons of the Beach and played Carolina Beach Music and oldies all over the Southeast and beyond. The Lowrys moved back to Mount Airy in 1997 and entered the local music scene again. There is an annual Jimmy Lowry Scholarship Concert hosted by the Surry Arts Council.

Live Theatre & Performers:

NoneSuch Playmakers...a community theatre group www.nonesuchplaymakers.com

Voce...of Mount Airy, a choral ensemble www.vocemtairy.org

Bluegrass and Old Time Music Jams...are held nightly around the county email randy@mtairychamber.org for locations/times

Venues include **The Andy Griffith Playhouse, The Earl Theatre,** and **The Blackmon Amphitheater**: all part of The Surry Arts Council www.surryarts.org; and the **Mount Airy Public Library** provides live entertainment https://nwrlibrary.org/mountairy/; and **The Cherry Orchard Theatre** provides outdoor performances in August www.leveringorchard.com/virginia-outdoor-theatre.

Local churches provide live theatre periodically throughout the year and **weekly performances** are scheduled at the local vineyards, restaurants, and bars.

The Mount Airy Visitor Center 200 North Main, 800-948-0949 provides an updated weekly schedule of events. Drop by and ask for a copy or call for one to be mailed or emailed.

Metal Artist...Chazz Elstone is an artist who specializes in metalwork sculptures, most of which have a biblical meaning. Visitors are invited to walk through the sculpture garden on his property down to the Fern Glen Chapel, which is a wooded area filled with more sculptures covered in ferns down by a creek. The path winds through an acre and a half of his property. **Scoops Ice Cream,** owned by Elstone, is located on the property. Nine miles from Main Street (near I77) 5091 West Pine Street, Mount Airy

Miss Angel's Farm...The Farm is near Exit 100 on I 77, located just off Hwy 89. It is a pick-your-own peaches, blackberries, flowers, and pumpkins farm. A country store with homemade ice cream, canned goods, and vegetables is located on the grounds. A flourishing greenhouse provides an abundance of flowers and plants. They host several events each year: Spring Picnic in the Orchard, Ole Fashioned Hoe Down, Peach Festival, Adult Pizza Making, Oktoberfest, Thanksgiving Apple Pie Workshop, Christmas on the Orchard, and dinner shows. Added to these events, is the Pick Your Own Days from June through October. At the end of harvest, there is a seasonal corn maze.

The child-friendly farm has a petting zoo, a play area, tractor rides, and barrel rides. During the scheduled events, you can bring a picnic basket and enjoy the day on the farm or buy prepared food. Their farm is the source of the fresh fruits and vegetables used in their bakery.

www.missangelsheavenlypiesinc.com

Mount Airy Autism Society...Meets the last Thursday of every month at the Salvation Army 615 S South Street. Their annual walk to benefit the society is in April. Autism Spectrum Disorder (ASD) is known as a "spectrum" disorder because there is a wide variation in type and symptoms an individual may have.

Mount Airy City Schools...The city schools have received local, district, state, and national awards. The city school system was one of the first in the state to go full-time during the 2020 pandemic and served as a model for the state. Mount Airy has two Christian schools and one charter school.

www.mtairy.k12.nc.us

Old-Time Fiddler's Convention...The Annual Mount Airy Old-Time Fiddlers Convention at Veterans Memorial Park in Mount Airy, North Carolina is traditionally held the first weekend in June. This family-friendly event brings together musicians and fans for two full days of competition, jam sessions, dancing, singing, education, and family entertainment. This popular festival, established in 1972, is dedicated to old-time and bluegrass music, as well as dance. The Fiddlers Convention features solo and band competitions whose winners are awarded cash prizes. Primitive and full hookup campsites are available.

Outdoor Recreation...Surry County offers four rivers, and 100s of miles of canoe/kayak streams with over 20 river access points. It has 36 miles of stocked trout waters. The Surry Scenic Bikeway has over 500 miles with 8 loops and 18 miles of mountain bike trails and more than 25 miles of horseback trails. Within the parks, you have a public pool, splash pad, and skateboard Park.

One of the better outdoor features is Mount Airy's proximity to three State Parks, and 15 minutes from the Blue Ridge Parkway.

There are over 2,000 acres of hunting and game lands, 4

golf country clubs, 4-disc golf courses, 6 RV Campgrounds, with tent options, 21 wineries, 4 breweries, and 1 distillery. www.surryedp.com

Pickleball Courts...Mount Airy has three dedicated outdoor pickleball courts at Riverside Park 350 Riverside Drive. Indoor courts are lined at Reeves Community Center 113 South Renfro Street and Northern Wellness and Fitness Center 280 North Point Boulevard. Some local churches also have courts. Mount Airy is home to the annual Mayberry Pickleball Tournament, usually held in July. Mount Airy has become a Pickleball destination.

Restaurant Row...Restaurant Row is located on Rockford Street Extension (HWY 601). Starting with Highway 55 Restaurant and going to Walmart, for approximately one mile toward Dobson, there are 31 restaurants, along with hotels and shopping.

On the two and 1/2 mile stretch from South 52 Bypass at Chile Rojo Mexican Restaurant to North 52 Bypass at Coach's Neighborhood Grill, there are another 12 restaurants.

On business 52, from the Derby Restaurant to the Gondola Italian Restaurant there are 23.

Near downtown, on Lebanon Street is the historic Dairy Center, Ocie's, and Porky's Bar B Q

In addition, there are numerous restaurants located around town and in the county.

From downtown, within five (5) minutes you have a choice of more than 67 restaurants.

Retirement Communities/Nursing Facilities...Listed in no specific order are the Colonial Care, Assisted Living; Central Care Assisted Living; Central Continuing Care Nursing Home; Dunmore Plantation Assisted Living; Northern Surry SNF Skilled Nursing; Ridgecrest Retirement Community: Riverwood Assisted Living, Dobson; Surry Community Health and Rehabilitation Center Nursing Home; and Twelve Oaks, Assisted Living.

Rockford...Founded in 1790, it was Surry County's first county seat, and today is the home of a true old-fashioned country store and restaurant. You can buy a Grape Nehi or Orange Crush (both sodas made popular in the 1930s) and have a seat on one of the front porch benches or grab a rocking chair and let your imagination roam to former days.

Siamese Twins...Eng and Chang were born in the village of Meklong, Siam (now Thailand), on May 11, 1811. For their entire lives, the twins were connected at the chest. On April 1, 1829, at the age of 18, they left Siam with the approval of their mother and the King of Siam. The twins earned money for themselves and their agents by making appearances throughout the United States, Canada, Central America, Cuba, and Europe. They became popular celebrities. In 1832, having fulfilled all contract obligations they became independent and toured on their own. When they became American citizens in 1839, they honored their friend, Fred Bunker by using the surname Bunker.

They traveled to North Carolina and settled in Wilkes County. They had amassed a considerable amount of money. They met the Yates sisters and married them, Adelaide, and Sarah on April 13, 1843. The two families produced twenty-one children.

They moved to Mount Airy in 1845. In 1857, they built a second home and began their system of three days in one house followed by three days in the other – with each brother being the master of his own home. They observed this routine until they died on January 17, 1874, at the age of 62.

Sarah is buried in an unmarked grave on their property with some of the children and slaves. Eng and Chang's bodies were buried on the property near the home. They were moved in 1917 and buried by Adelaide at White Plains Baptist Church. Their story continues to fascinate the public.

Many books and a play is written about them. Hundreds

of descendants continue to host a reunion the last weekend in July each year in Mount Airy. A display is at the Surry Arts Council. Their graves at the Church are about 3 ½ miles from downtown, on the way, you can see a home they built and be in the area of the Mayberry Campground, which is owned by a descendant.

Sonker...Sonker dessert is unique to Surry County and is like a pot pie or a cobbler. It is a blend of fruit and unshaped dough sweetened with sugar or sorghum cane molasses. Popular fruits include blackberries, peaches, sweet potatoes, and apples. Folklore tells us that people in the area made sonker to stretch the usage of fruit in tough times. There are area variations, some have dumplings, while others are like pies. www.sonkertrail.org

Sonker Festival...The Sonker Festival is held each year on the first Saturday of October at the Edwards-Franklin House from 1 - 5 PM - rain (not hurricanes) or shine. It features the deep-dish pie, known as sonker, displays of local crafts and historical collections as well as traditional music performed by musicians from the area. The event is presented by the Surry County Historical Society. The event is free but there is a small charge for the sonker and beverage.

www.sonkertrail.org, www.surryhistoricalsociety.org

Sports and Game Venues...Mount Airy offers a variety of sports and game venues. Both the Starlite Skate Center and Hardy's Custom Mini Golf course are popular.

Reeves Community Center and Northern Health are two full-service gyms. Any Time Fitness is open 24 hours a day and located at 844 North Main Street.

PrimeTime Performance is a sports training facility.

Ridzo Athletics is a Crossfit Facility.

Popular board and video game shops in the area include Paradise Games, GameStop, and Game Collectors.

Carolina Ziplines are only 30 minutes from downtown. 336- 972-7656

Westwood Park and local wineries have disc golf. Pickleball courts, basketball courts, playground, soccer fields, canoe/kayak launches, and the greenway are located at Riverside Park.

Surry Arts Council...The Surry Arts Council provides high-quality experiences in performing and visual arts. Shows and events are scheduled throughout the year including The Blue Ridge & Beyond concerts, which feature numerous nationally known performers. Beach music and more are featured at the Summer Concert Series, at the Blackmon Amphitheatre, located downtown.

The live theatre performed at the Andy Griffith Playhouse provides a variety of entertaining plays and musicals. Annually, they host music festivals, summer concerts, retreats, and a variety of other shows and entertainers.

The Arts Council's schedule includes weekly painting, dance, and drama classes as well as new offerings held throughout the year. Each summer they offer creative and fun summer camps. They offer free music and dance lessons weekly www.surryarts.org

Surry Community College...Located in the beautiful foothills of North Carolina, the two-year College was founded in 1964 and serves Surry and Yadkin counties. Annually, the College serves 3,200 students seeking certificates, diplomas, or degrees in a wide range of curriculum programming. Additionally, it serves 18,000 students through the Workforce, Technology, and Community Education Division. www.surry.edu

Veteran's Park...The park has a campground from primitive to full hookups located at 691 West Lebanon Street, about 1 ½ miles from the center of downtown. The Park sponsors three major events each year: The Bluegrass and Old-Time Fiddlers Convention, held the first Friday and Saturday in June; the Surry County Agricultural Fair in September; and a Giant Flea market the weekend of the

Autumn Leaves Festival. Car shows and other events are scheduled at different times during the year. www.veteransparkmtairy.org

White Sulfur Springs Resort...Built-in the late 1890s, the old White Sulphur Springs Hotel, was a grand resort that boasted of, among other things, a mineral spring — that was guaranteed to cure whatever ailed you. People seeking its curative waters still come to the spring. The resort provided the perfect mountain location, comfortable weather, easy access to the railroad, and the magical spring. Today, a wedding and events venue sits where the hotel once stood. Cabins, catering, and activities are available. The event center is located 3 ½ miles from downtown. 336-786-6769   133 White Sulfur Springs Road, Mount Airy

Wineries...Surry County is the birthplace of the Yadkin Valley American Viticultural Area (AVA). The Surry County Wine Trail features 21 wineries.

The Blue Ridge foothills sit at an ideal elevation and latitude for growing European vinifera grapes. Roughly three-fourths are classic vinifera varietals for dry and semi-sweet wines, setting the Yadkin Valley apart from other wine regions in the South. Sweeter wines are available.

Lodging and touring options are available. Wineries with on-site accommodations: Carolina Heritage, Elkin Creek, Grassy Creek, Haze Gray, Hidden Vineyard, JOLO, Pilot Mountain Vineyards, Round Peak, Serre Vineyards, Shelton Vineyards, Slightly Askew, and Stony Knoll. Events, dining, and other activities are in many of the wineries/vineyards. www.yadkinvalleync.com

Appendix IV

Famous People from Mount Airy

(This is not an inclusive list, there are more famous people and some infamous, and others are becoming famous.)

Joe Bill Adams...NASCAR driver

Larry Alderman (1952 -)...American Songwriter and Musician *Americana & Real Good Feel Good Song*

Frank Beamer (1946 -)...head football coach Virginia Tech

Ron Blackburn (1935 – 1998)...Major League Baseball player

Chang and Eng Bunker (1811 – 1874)...internationally famous showmen, the original Siamese Twins

General Henry Wolfe Butner (1875-1937)...WWI general

Ben Callahan (1957 – 2007)...Major League Baseball player

Jack Childress...ACC Football Referee, Head Referee Orange Bowl, Sugar Bowl, Rose Bowl, and the National Championship Game

Libby Childress...43rd Scripps National Spelling Bee Champion

Tyson Clabo...NFL offensive tackle who moved here

Rick Clifton...DreamWorks Creative Audio-Visual Director and has won a Day Time Emmy. He produces trailers and does some acting

Donald Wayne Collins (1936-2021)...NASCAR driver and well-known local pastor

Bill Cox (1929-2017)...played football for Duke and Washington Red Skins

Chubby Dean (1916–1970)...Major League Baseball player

Debbie Severs Diamont...former weather person on WXII, and career educator who influenced many

Easter Brothers (Russell, James, and Ed)...nationally known gospel music artists, who won many awards

Jeff and Sherry Easter...two-time Grammy-nominated and multi-award-winning artists including two Dove Awards

Ralph Epperson (1921-2006)...owner of WPAQ (broadcasts the 2nd longest-running radio show in the country)

Donna Fargo (1945 -)...country music singer/songwriter with 10 number-one hits in the 1970s, including *Happiest Girl in the USA*

Chris Fleming...NASCAR sportsman series driver

Luke Fleming...NASCAR sportsman series driver

Frank Fleming...NASCAR sportsman series driver

Benton Flippen (1920 – 2011)...old-time fiddler, banjo player, and guitarist

John Floyd...Comedian

Jesse Franklin...20th governor of North Carolina

Maddie Gardner (1993 -)...local news reporter and internationally recognized cheerleader

Andy Griffith (1926 – 2012)...American male actor

Ron Hall...Invented the headset system used at fast food restaurants to take orders. He is a local historian from our bordering county in Virginia but chose to retire in Mount Airy

Bill Hayes...television producer

Caleb Vance Haynes (1895-1996)...USAF Major General and grandson of Chang Bunker (one of the Siamese Twins)

Earl Hatcher...NASCAR driver and Official

Jerry Hemmings (1948 -)...basketball coach

Melva Houston (1949-2020)...highly acclaimed jazz vocalist, and blues and gospel singer

Tommy Jarrell (1901 – 1985)...old-time fiddler, banjo player, and singer

Jan Kriska... In 2017, Dr. Kriska was the only person to complete the 1000-mile Iditasport Extreme event in Alaska in 29 days, 20 hours, and 20 minutes and he pulled all his 70 lb gear in a sled. Only 15 people have ever completed

Luke Lambert...NASCAR crew chief

William Liebenow (1920-2017)...PT Boat Skipper who rescued Kennedy

Ken Lowe...owner of the Home and Garden channel

Betty Lynn (1926 -2021)...Actress

Mark Daniel Merritt (1961-)...American music composer

Sam Moir (1924-2018)...Legendary basketball coach, Catawba College and professional baseball player and recipient of the Purple Heart

Ted McBride...Deaflympics, silver/bronze medalist

Billy Oakley...Dirt Racing Champion

"Old-time" music...Round Peak genre began in Surry County with musicians Charlie Lowe, Tommy Jarrell, Fred Cockerham, and many more

Maddy O'Reilly (1990 -)...pornographic actress

Roy H. Park (1910-1993)...created Duncan Hines brand

Kathryn Smith Reynolds (1880-1924)...wife of tycoon RJ Reynolds

George Sappenfield...Designed the first competitive disc golf course and responsible for the development of disc golf as it is played today

Zack Sievers (1984 -)...Hollywood Sound Mixer/Supervisor Nomadland & Primetime Emmy Award for *Gettysburg*

Summer Shelton...movie and television producer

Alex Sink...former chief financial officer for Florida, and Democratic nominee for governor (2010)

Christopher Stolz...combat and professional photographer

Paul Webster...Brigadier one-star General US Reserves
Anna Wood (1985 -)...actress

Appendix V

Reflections for Personal or Group Study

Blessing

1.What are the most valuable blessings in your life?
2.What do you feel prevents people from seeing their blessings?
3.How do gratitude and thankfulness enhance your life?
4.How can you show gratitude for your blessings?
5.Describe the value of lifelong friends:
6.What role does luck, commitment, and goal setting play in blessings?
7.Discuss Deuteronomy 28:2 And all these blessings shall come upon you and overtake you, if you obey the voice of the Lord your God.

Calling

1.Discuss how each person has a "calling" in life?
2.How can you discover your calling?
3.How do you feel you can cultivate your calling?
4.Think back on your childhood. What were some hints/signs that helped identify your calling?
5.What tries to deter your calling? How did you overcome and remain focused?
6.Observe. Do you see anything in a child in your life that hints at what their calling may be? If so, how can you support them in fulfilling their destiny?
7.Discuss Jeremiah 29:11 I know the plans I have for you declares the Lord, plans to prosper you and not harm you, plans to give you hope and a future.

Calm

1.What role did DNA and environment play in whom you have become?

2.Discuss how meekness and remaining calm is strength.

3.How can you learn to benefit from positive influences?

4.How do you choose to be meek, humble, or calm?

5.What does "preferring one another" mean? How does that make you feel?

6.List old-timey sayings you can share with those you love:

7.Discuss John 14:27 Peace I leave with you, My peace I give to you. Let not your hearts be troubled, neither let them be afraid.

Charity

1.What is charity?

2.How can you show charity?

3.What childhood experiences helped make you who you are today?

4.Have you or do you know someone who has had an experience with angels? If yes, would you share?

5.How were angels used in the Bible?

6.Do you think each of us has a destiny? If yes, how do we reach our destiny?

7.Discuss Psalm 91:11 He will command His angels concerning you to guard you in all your ways.

Community

1.What is community?

2.What is small-town community – is it different?

3.Discuss how small-town community can be found anywhere?

4.What can you do to build the best community?

5.Is community inclusive – are there disadvantages in community?

6.What are the benefits of small-town community?

7.Discuss Romans 12:5 In Christ we, though many, form one body and each member belongs to all the others.

Compassion

1. Discuss compassion and empathy:
2. Can you grow in compassion, if so, how?
3. Do you think you have innate qualities that contribute to community, if so, what are they?
4. Are there pains or hurts in your life that need attention, if yes, what positive step(s) can you take?
5. How can your past help others?
6. Discuss the Golden Rule and compassion:
7. Discuss Lamentations 3:22-23 Because of the Lord's great love, we are not consumed, for His compassions never fail. They are new every morning; great is Your faithfulness.

Connected

1. What are your thoughts about the power of life connections?
2. How can you nurture connections?
3. What have been some of the most powerful connections for you over time?
4. Imagine and describe the loss of being without sincere connections?
5. Who would you like to connect with?
6. Describe how you connect with music:
7. Discuss Ephesians 4:16 From whom the whole body, being fitted and held together by what every joint supplies, according to the proper working of each individual part, causes the growth of the body for the building itself up in love.

Dream

1. Discuss how someone's past might be a roadblock to someone's dream:
2. List ways to overcome roadblocks to dreams:
3. Do you have a dream? If yes, what are your first steps toward your dream?
4. Do you have roadblocks to your dream or is your past a roadblock? If yes, how do you overcome?

5.What is the importance of looking in the "mirror" when reaching for your dream?

6.How can you support someone's dream?

7.Discuss Psalm 20:4 May he give you the desire of your heart and make all your plans succeed.

Encouraging

1.Who are the encouragers in your life?

2.Who have you encouraged to make life changes?

3.Can you encourage yourself? If yes, how?

4.What are specific things you can do to be an encourager?

5.Is it important to encourage children? If yes, how do you encourage children?

6.Can you give specific examples of how someone has been encouraged, either personally or someone you know?

7.Discuss Romans 15:2 Each of us should please our neighbors for their good, to build them up.

Family

1.How important is family to you?

2.What makes a family?

3.If a family is not connected, what steps can be taken to help a family connect?

4.Discuss family events, reunions, or other gatherings that provide opportunities to build family connections.

5.Have you hosted or attended a large family event? If so, discuss your experience.

6.What are modern-day barriers, preventing families from being connected?

7.Discuss Psalm 133:1 Look at how good and pleasing it is when families live together as one.

Friend

1.Describe the characteristics of a friend:

2.Describe how you are a good friend:

3.List your true friend(s):   What makes them true

friends?

4.Do you think everyone can be your friend? Why or why not?

5.Why do people need friends?

6.What does Proverbs mean by stating "a friend that sticks closer than a brother"?

7.Discuss Proverbs 27:9 Perfume and incense bring joy to the heart, and the pleasantness of a friend springs from their heartfelt advice.

Hope

1.What does the statement "I'm still riding hope" mean to you?

2.What is hope?

3.How do you overcome hopelessness?

4.Can you give hope – if so, how?

5.Can you lose hope – if so, how?

6.The Psalmist said, the Lord is my hope – what does that mean?

7.Discuss Isaiah 40:31 Those who hope in the Lord will renew their strength. They will soar on wings like eagles, they will run and not grow weary, they will walk and not faint.

Imagination

1.What is imagination?

2.Who are the storytellers in your life?

3.Recall a story/experience that allowed your imagination to create:

4.What is your story that ignites imagination?

5.Who or what spurs imagination in your life?

6.Does everyone have imagination?

7.Discuss I Corinthians 2:9 Things which the eye has not seen, and the ear has not heard, and which have not entered the heart of man, All that God has prepared for them that love Him.

Influence

1.List influencers in your life?

2.Name persons you are influencing.

3.How powerful is influence?

4.How do you gain influencers in your life?

5.How can you be an influencer?

6.How do you become an influencer?

7.Discuss Proverbs 27:17 Iron sharpens iron, and one man sharpens another.

Kindness

1.List acts of kindness:

2.Identify and describe three people you know who demonstrate kindness.

3.What is your earliest memory of someone showing you kindness?

4.How do you think kindness changes/develops people?

5.Why do you think some people are unkind?

6.How do you become a kind person?

7.Discuss Galatians 6:9-10 Be kind to one another, tenderhearted, forgiving one another, as God in Christ forgave you.

Laughter

1.Describe someone you know who has a lot of laughter, how do they make you feel?

2.What is the difference between laughing with someone and laughing at someone?

3.When might laughter be inappropriate?

4.Why do you think some people do not laugh or like others to laugh?

5.Think of a truly funny story, share it with others.

6.How would you describe your laughter?

7.Discuss Proverbs 17:22 A cheerful heart is good medicine, but a broken spirit saps a person's strength.

Loyalty

1.Define loyalty.

2.Describe people you know who are loyal.

3.Identity your loyal friends, what makes them loyal?

4.Discuss a time when being loyal was important but

challenging.

5.How can we be a loyal friend?

6.Who or what should we be loyal to?

7.Discuss Proverbs 18:24 A man of many companions may come to ruin, but there is a friend who sticks closer than a brother.

Neighborly Love

1.List ways you can show neighborly love:

2.Describe a time when someone demonstrated neighborly love:

3.Who is your neighbor?

4.List challenges to being a good neighbor:

5.Discuss your thoughts about the statement, 'good neighbors are more easily found in small communities.'

6.Does being a good neighbor look different in a large city, if so, how?

7.Discuss I Thessalonians 5:11 Encourage one another, and build each other up, just as in fact you are doing.

Optimistic

1.How do you develop the skill of optimism?

2.Describe a time when optimism helped you through a crisis:

3.Can you identify a time in your life that taught you a lesson and helped you be more optimistic?

4.What faith statement is your anchor through life?

5.How do you feel when you are around optimistic people?

6.How do pessimistic people become more positive?

7.Discuss Romans 8:28 We know that for those who love God, all things work together for good, for those who are called according to his purpose

Push

1.Who and how have people encouraged (pushed) you to fulfill your purpose?

2.Identify and describe how you are encouraging

someone to fulfill their destiny.

3.How can you become a better encourager?

4.How do you know if you are 'pushing' someone too much?

5.How can you push yourself to accomplishments?

6.Discuss how you might 'push' a child/youth; how is it different from pushing an adult?

7.Discuss Hebrews 10:24 And let us consider how we may spur one another on toward love and good deeds.

Resilience

1.How would you define or describe resilience?

2.What contributes to building resilience?

3.Why do you think some people give up?

4.Can we help people become resilient? If so, how?

5.Can you give examples of people with resilience?

6.When has being resilient been beneficial to you?

7.Discuss Philippians 4:13 I can do all things through Christ which strengthens me.

Sugar

1.Do you have sweet memories of a grandparent, parent, or someone in your life who was an important part of your life? If so, describe them.

2.Why do some people become bitter because of difficult losses while others become sweet and nice?

3.What are positive ways to respond to loss?

4.Why does it seem that some people experience more loss or challenges in life than others?

5.Identify ways to avoid inappropriate language while responding to difficult situations.

6.What are sayings/words people say to soften a conversation.

7.Discuss Proverbs 16:24 Pleasant words are a honeycomb, sweet to the soul and healing to the bones.

Survive

1. What is a survivor?
2. What is needed to survive challenging situations?
3. Discuss how some struggles are harder than others.
4. What, if any, are the lasting effects of being a survivor?
5. How is survival a part of everyone's life?
6. Discuss if there are different skills needed to survive adversity as a child, teenager, adult, or an older person?
7. Discuss II Corinthians 4:8-9 We are afflicted in every way, but not crushed, perplexed, but not driven to despair; persecuted, but not forsaken; struck down, but not destroyed.

Tragedy

1. Why do you think tragedy strikes?
2. What lesson do you think tragedy can teach?
3. How do you learn from tragedy?
4. Can tragedy be avoided?
5. How can we help someone facing tragic situations?
6. Do some people experience tragedy more than others, and if so, why?
7. Discuss Psalm 46:1 God is our refuge and strength, a very present help in the time of trouble.

Wisdom

1. Discuss knowledge and wisdom:
2. How do you develop wisdom?
3. Identify opportunities in your life where wisdom can be applied:
4. List inspiring wisdom statements:
5. Who are the wise people in your life, and why?
6. How can you apply James 3:17?
7. Discuss Proverbs 16:16 How much better to get wisdom than gold, to get insight rather than silver.

Index

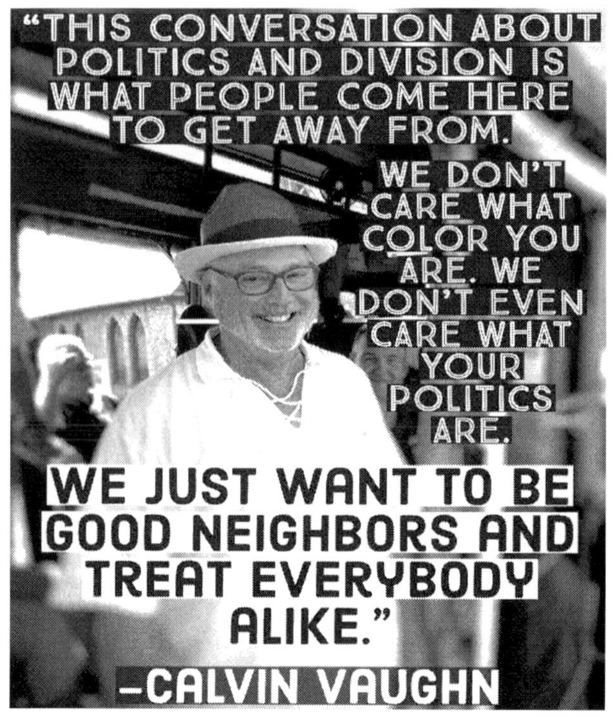

About the Author

Calvin B. Vaughn, Jr. lives in Mount Airy, North Carolina, where he is a retired recreation director, former pastor, and more than 35 years in the tourist industry. He is the owner of Fun Thyme Travel Company and is one of the more experienced and entertaining tour guides in the business. He is a public speaker and writer. He has been writing for his own pleasure for 40 years. Since 1982, his articles have appeared in local newspapers, senior aging publications, and a state magazine. His latest short story was published in 2019. He reveres small-town charm and loves living in and telling everyone about Mount Airy – the best small town in America.

Geoffrey Walker

The front cover design of the book was created by Geoffrey Walker. Geoffrey grew up in the small town of Elkin, NC, part of Surry County. He loves art and making it. He owns a small shop called Demo's Art Loft, located in Elkin. He is often seen in the Mount Airy Arts and Entertainment District displaying his work. Contact Geoffrey at 336-944-9939 or demosartloft@outlook.com

Robbie Curlee

The Cover Photograph

The cover is a photograph of MAin Street, Mount Airy, NC and taken by Robbie Curlee. Robbie is our unofficial town photographer. He captures the beauty of everyday events. He is often seen with camera in hand in our downtown. He and Suzanne, his wife, are from South Carolina. Loving Mount Airy, they visited for 20 years before moving here. He is a retired Civil Engineer. Photography and "All things Mayberry" are two of his favorite things. The Curlees are perfect neighbors with a small-town charm. Follow him on Facebook and you will see the beauty he captures from scenes all over town.

Made in the USA
Middletown, DE
09 May 2023

29970859R00130